Praise for *Chronicle of the Left Hand*

"There are many extraordinary, untold moments in black American history that are now being uncovered and that of James Lloydovich Patterson is one of them. What makes it so special is that he was born and grew up in Stalin's Russia, where his father had immigrated in the 1930s in search of greater equality and work opportunities. Published in English for the first time, *Chronicle of the Left Hand*—which appeared in Russian in 1964—is Patterson's paternal grandmother's account of her grinding life of poverty in Virginia during the dark days of the Ku Klux Klan lynch mobs and how her son—Patterson's father, Lloyd—made the brave decision during the Great Depression to travel to the Soviet Union for a better life and a new beginning: 'This country was working wonders. Lloyd had found himself here.' For the oppressed and persecuted African American, Soviet Russia ironically offered a refuge. As a child, Patterson starred in a popular propaganda film—*Circus*—that extolled the virtues of Soviet racial tolerance. He was lionized and became an unexpected star, but he had to come to terms with living through the most oppressive period in Soviet history, when many Russians were enduring the terrors of the Stalinist purges. Nevertheless, Patterson enjoyed a successful career in the Soviet Navy before turning to poetry, eventually immigrating to the USA in the 1990s.

"Included in the book is project coordinator Amy Ballard's account of her encounters with the aging and reclusive Patterson, who now lives in Washington, DC, a discussion of his life and film stardom in Russia, and many of his fascinating personal photographs. Together they provide an unusual and moving tribute to an extraordinary and courageous black family and offer revealing insights into a still little known episode in the history of blacks in the Soviet Union."

—Helen Rappaport, *Sunday Times* and *New York Times* bestselling author, *After the Romanovs* and *In Search of Mary Seacole: The Making of a Cultural Icon*

"The Patterson family story weaves through the labyrinth of American race relations from slavery to a present when older African Americans all too often find themselves shuffled off to the periphery of society (as, sadly, are elderly compatriots of all hues). The saga of James Lloydovich Patterson, though, detours to the Soviet Union in all of its own complexity. Among the Soviet Union's most famous personages, Patterson tries to navigate his own way as a Russian-born black man through the contradictions of Stalin's and later Brezhnev's Soviet Union. A submarine officer, a recognized poet, and the son of a well-regarded artist, he searches for his own path, one that eventually leads him to a Washington, DC, subsidized apartment. Combining background essays and the translation of Patterson's grandmother's Soviet published memoirs about black life after the American Civil War, *Chronicle of the Left Hand* is a story about the resilience of the human spirit, affectionately compiled by the many very different admirers of James Patterson as well as by James Patterson himself."

—Blair A. Ruble, Distinguished Fellow, Woodrow Wilson International Center for Scholars; author of *The Muse of Urban Delirium* and *Proclaiming Presence from the Washington Stage*

Chronicle of the Left Hand

Chronicle of the Left Hand

An American Black Family's Story from Slavery to Russia's Hollywood

James Lloydovich Patterson

NEW ACADEMIA PUBLISHING · SCARITH

Washington, DC

Library of Congress Control Number: 2022931374
ISBN 979-8-9852214-1-1 (alk. paper)

 SCARITH is an imprint of New Academia Publishing

 New Academia Publishing
4401-A Connecticut Ave. NW #236, Washington DC 20008
info@newacademia.com - www.newacademia.com

Note

This is the first translation in English. This English version is line edited, and some text has been added or deleted to assist with text clarity; some text additions have been explained in the endnotes.

The article "The Pattersons: Expatriate and Native Son" by Rimgaila Salys was originally published in the *Russian Review* July 2016, volume 75, issue 3. The article, which has been updated for this book, uses the ALA-LC transliteration scheme. Reprinted courtesy of John Wiley and Sons and Rimgaila Salys.

All illustrations in this book come courtesy of James L. Patterson with the exception of:

Figure 2: Westfield Historical Society, Westfield, New Jersey

Figure 24: Museum of Komsomolsk-on-Amur, Russia

Figure 30: Suzanne Tolstoy

Front Cover: James Lloydovich Patterson with his grandmother Margaret Glascoe, Moscow, c. 1937

Back Cover: Poster by Boris Zelensky, *Tsirk*, 1936, Mosfilm, Moscow, Russian Federation

Author photograph by Katya Chilingiri Balaban, Washington, DC, April 2021

Contents

Publisher's Note

During the years of Stalin's Great Terror, amid famine, arrests, forced labor, mock trials, and executions, the government of the Soviet Union turned to cinema as a means to distract the masses from the grim reality of the day. Cinema had been a powerful tool for indoctrination and control since 1918, when Lenin himself declared that "Cinema is for us the most important of all the arts."

In the mid-1930s, the strategy was to produce "movies for the millions," entertaining to the populace and, at the same time, conveying the canons of Soviet ideology. The idea was to create a "Soviet Hollywood" on the model of popular genres, such as the western and the musical, but with scripts solidly rooted in Socialist Realist values.

The official entrusted with this task was Boris Shumyatsky, a Party *apparatchik* and head of the Cinema Ministry (GOSKINO). For a short period (1933-1938), he was successful in implementing the plan. But then his fortune changed and, like for many exponents of the arts and industry, his career ended abruptly with an arrest.

Most of the films produced during Shumyatsky's tenure were big hits with the viewers and drew huge audiences. Among them was *Circus*, "the greatest favorite of the time and also the greatest box-office success in the history of Soviet Cinema" (Neya Zorkaya, *Illustrated History of Soviet Cinema*, 1989).

Circus boosted the national pride with its we-are-better-than-the-West self-congratulatory thrust. Better still, it delighted the viewers with a spectacular *mise-en-scène*, circus acrobatics, "Rockettes" ballets, fancy costumes, and romantic rendezvous in glamorous skyscrapers suites. Grigory Alexandrov, as the film director and former assistant director to Eisenstein, endowed the film with high production values.

But what greatly contributed to its success was the emergence of the star system—a firmament of popular actors with whom the viewers could identify, and be transported into a fake world of socialist delights. The greatest star of that period was Lyubov Orlova, often called "the prima donna of Soviet cinema" and compared to Marlene Dietrich and Greta Garbo. She was Alexandrov's wife and played the lead role in all of his musicals.

As part of the *nomenklatura*, movie stars enjoyed a privileged position. Privileged but precarious. In fact, privileges and stardom could be suddenly terminated, together with their beneficiaries. A notorious case in point is the assassination of Jewish actor Solomon Mikhoels in 1948, on Stalin's orders. Mikhoels played a supporting character in *Circus*, but his demise has nothing to do with the film. This case is mentioned here to underline the discrepancy between fantasy and reality—while anti-racist lullabies from the screen stirred feelings of sentimental complacency in the viewers, anti-semitism was festering in politics and society, like it had since czarist times.

Little James Patterson became an instant star in the Soviet movie world, on and off the screen, and had the good fortune of maintaining his privileged position throughout his adult life, before moving to the United States.

The story of the Patterson family, recounted in this book, presents an aspect of the Soviet reality which the majority of ordinary citizens have never enjoyed. For this reason, it is a story worth telling.

Anna Lawton, February 2022

Now I must tell you that my whole life has been happiness. Through all of the misfortunes, etc., I did not plan anything. Life was there for me and I accepted it. And life, whatever came out, has been beautiful, and I love everybody.

—*Louis Armstrong*

Introduction

This English translation of *Chronicle of the Left Hand* is a love letter—a love letter to James Lloydovich Patterson from the many people who made this book a reality.

The book blossomed from roots planted years before during a lecture on black Americans who had moved to the Soviet Union to better their lives. The lecturer told the story of Mr. Patterson, the child actor and later poet who won so many hearts in the hugely popular 1936 Soviet film *Circus* [*Tsirk*] when he was three years old. She mentioned that he lived in Washington, DC, which also happened to be—and remains—my home. As I left the lecture at the National Museum of African Art that day, I filed the fact that James Patterson and I were "neighbors" in the back of my mind.

In more recent years, having retired with emerita status from the Smithsonian Institution, where I reviewed building-design projects for historic preservation compliance, I've pursued varied interests. So it was in July 2020, cooped up at home because of COVID-19 stay-at-home restrictions and on the internet constantly, that I read with fascination an article in the *Los Angeles Review of Books* entitled "The Only One Left: A Conversation with James Lloydovich Patterson about Grigori Aleksandrov's *Circus*."

"The Only One Left"—*Wow*, I thought. Of this famous Soviet film about a white American circus performer who has a black son, both of whom are shunned by Americans but embraced by the Soviets, Mr. Patterson was the only surviving main cast member. At that moment, I realized how special it was that he still graced this earth and how fortunate I was to reside so close to a living legend. I recalled the museum lecture from so many years before and, considering the historic importance of Mr. Patterson, his experience, his family, and advanced age—he is well into his eighties—and with time on my hands, I wanted to meet him. After some online research, I found contact information for the article's author, Professor Sasha Razor of the University of California, Los Angeles, and reached out to her. I had read that Mr. Patterson, though once a celebrated star in Russia, had become a recluse in his adopted home of the US, so I asked the professor if he received visitors. She informed me that he did and arranged for me to visit the aged poet at his apartment in DC.

It's here that I should mention that my intrigue with Russia goes back to when I was a teen, sparked by Robert K. Massie's book *Nicholas and Alexandra* about the last tsar and tsarina of Russia; and though I have read numerous books and articles on Russia and seen many documentaries, I had never heard of Mr. Patterson or the film *Circus* before that National Museum of African Art lecture. My undertaking of the topic of black Americans fleeing the US for the Soviet Union in the early part of the twentieth century had only begun on the day of that museum discussion; now, I was anxious to learn more.

With a home address and introduction in hand, I looked forward to the impending visit with the hermitic star, but the thought of it made me nervous too. After all, I was about to meet James Lloydovich Patterson, the most famous black child actor in Russian history. My nerves and the fact that I wasn't sure about his English—I only speak about two words of Russian—prompted me to bring along support in the form of my friend of more than forty years, Suzanne Tolstoy, who speaks Russian and is happy to keep me calm.

On a hot day in July, Suzanne and I walked toward Mr. Patterson's apartment building, set near a retail area in the midst of a modest DC neighborhood. We entered the government-subsidized building for seniors, and once at Mr. Patterson's door, his caretaker, wearing a mask, as were we, let us into his one-bedroom home. Immediately, we saw Mr. Patterson, also with a mask on, sitting on his sofa in his small living room. It was devoid of any pictures save for a dog-eared poster of *Circus* on one wall. We introduced ourselves. When Suzanne told him her last name, his eyes brightened. He asked, in English, how she might be related to the Russian author Leo Tolstoy. Suzanne shared that her late husband, Vladimir, was Tolstoy's grandnephew. Mr. Patterson visibly relaxed and told us that Lyubov Orlova, the star of *Circus* who had played his mother, had told him she'd met Leo Tolstoy when she was a child. The ice broken, we all proceeded to share a nice visit.

That afternoon, Mr. Patterson beautifully sang the famous lullaby from *Circus*—a song sung to his character Jimmy in the climactic scene where Soviet citizens embrace him—and talked about his mother and father, both of whom he still dearly missed years after their deaths. He also told us that he missed Russian food and good chocolate, which he had gorged on as a little boy. As his aging eyes sparkled from just mentioning that memory, I could see that he was not only the last one left from the movie but perhaps one of the last people left from his real life. With that, this man, who had suffered a stroke some years ago, took my heart. As a token of our appreciation for the visit, I gave him an art book depicting paintings of the Russian countryside and Suzanne gave him some Russian candy. After two hours, we left.

On the way out of the building, I shared with Suzanne that I would really like to visit Mr. Patterson again—I felt a tugging I could not escape. I felt so close to this frail man, though I couldn't pinpoint why. It couldn't possibly be because we share the same birthday—July 17—though that didn't hurt. I thought about our other similarity—like him, I was born to an American father living overseas; but that and our birthday is where our commonalities ended. My father, a white Air Force pilot stationed in Japan during the Korean War, enjoyed a good life in America. On the other hand, Mr. Patterson's father, Lloyd Patterson, had left the US for the Soviet Union not to fight a war for the US but to fight a different kind of war. As a black man, he had sought the equality and work opportunities he and other black American citizens could not find here. I reflected on the fact that though Mr. Patterson had enjoyed the privilege of being a film star, that experience was born from generational struggles that had played out on US shores. Now, he was enduring a struggle of his own—the challenge of largely spending his old age by himself. That thought hurt me. I knew that he deserved better. It made my fingers itch to pick up the phone to dial him. Soon after we first met, I called him to ask if I could see him again. Instantly, he said yes.

For months, I visited my new friend at his home every now and then, but I talked with him on the phone a lot. After we both received the COVID-19 vaccine, I began to see him in person with regularity. On trips to his apartment, sometimes with my friends and sometimes alone, Mr. Patterson—what I have called him since the day we met—shared many more stories about his life, leaving me more amazed and curious. Together, as we enjoyed gourmet Russian chocolate I would bring over, we pored over piles of his papers and poems from his time in DC, to which he and his mother, Vera Aralova, a white Russian, had immigrated to in the mid-1990s; he and his mother had come here seeking financial stability as a poet and painter, respectively. His father, a radio broadcaster, had died in 1942, several months after sustaining a concussion during a German bombing of Moscow.

Among the writings Mr. Patterson shared with me was a poem he wrote about the death of his mother, who died in 2001, and a photocopy of a letter that the Harlem Renaissance poet Langston Hughes had sent to his father. Hughes and Lloyd Patterson had traveled to the Soviet Union together, along with other black Americans, to participate in a film project in 1932. The film never materialized, but from that trip came Lloyd's marriage to Vera and their children. After my first few visits with Mr. Patterson, bereft of his mother, father, and all of those in Russia he was once close to, he had told me that he feared I would not return to see him. And at the end of each visit, even today, I wait for his constant refrain, "Don't forget me," to which I always respond, "Of course I won't. Mr. Patterson, I'll never forget you." Though some of his American family members that love him deeply would also travel to see him in DC, this feeling of being forgotten ran deep in his soul.

I wanted my friend to know that he was loved by many others, so not long after meeting him, I had set about finding people who knew him. With much pleasure, I reconnected him with several of his acquaintances in the US. One of them is Andrew "Andy" Leddy of DC, who has his own fascinating story about how he met Mr. Patterson and his mother. In the 1990s, Andy, an American then working in Russia, purchased a large portrait of a black man in a Moscow antique store. The staff told him that it pictured Mr. Patterson and explained to Andy that he was a famous actor. Andy, curious to know more, located Mr. Patterson's mother in Moscow and paid her a visit. Upon showing her the portrait, she informed him that Lloyd Patterson, Mr. Patterson's father, was in fact the one in the painting standing in a sharp brown suit as if to the manner born. Later in DC, Andy met Mr. Patterson too.

As I found more of Mr. Patterson's friends and associates in the US, I realized that my search needed to extend beyond these shores. I contacted Russian museums, the writers' advocacy group PEN Russia, the film studio Mosfilm, and GARF, the State Archive of the Russian Federation. Representatives from each one of these institutions responded and were happy to learn that Mr. Patterson was alive and well. Additionally, the fact that I had met him amazed friends of mine in Russia, a country I have visited many times because of my endless fascination with it. Several of these friends wrote him touching notes, expressing how they had loved him in *Circus* and were so glad to know he was doing well. One told him that he felt like he was touching Mr. Patterson's face through the act of writing to him. As Mr. Patterson read this letter, and all the others, his eyes lit up because he knew, finally, that people really had not forgotten him.

During this short time discovering friends new and old, Mr. Patterson was elected to membership in PEN Russia, which prompted people from all over Russia to write to the organization to ask how they could contact him. One man from Tatarstan wrote him several times. He remembered Mr. Patterson's visit to Tatarstan in the 1960s when the then-young writer had traveled there with other artists to share his poetry. The fan also sent him photos of those visits, inspiring a smile to once again glow and replace my friend's sometimes sad face. As the letters continually flowed, so did in-person visits from me and my friends.

While this entire experience unfurled, the contrast between Mr. Patterson's solitary life in DC and the fascinating, vibrant, respected life he once lived in Russia left me feeling that more Americans should know about this man and accord him the respect he is due. I and the new friends he had made here wondered aloud how we could make that happen. From those brainstorming sessions, we thought how wonderful it would be to see one of his works published in the US; this would be the fulfillment of a long-held dream of his, which I had learned much about over our many visits. Now, the challenge was to determine how to make it happen.

After some research, I sought out Professor Emerita Rimgaila Salys, of the Russian Program at the University of

Colorado Boulder, who had written about Mr. Patterson. The professor suggested his book *Chronicle of the Left Hand*, the memoir of the poet's paternal grandmother's life in the US—she was the daughter of an American man who had once been enslaved. The professor sent me the Russian edition, which is sprinkled with Mr. Patterson's commentary and carries his byline. I requested the services of professional translator Jennifer Sunseri, and after she converted the text to English, I saw what a treasure trove of information it held about an aspect of the black American experience after the end of slavery. I decided that this was the book suitable for American publication. Eventually, everything else fell into place.

In addition to her book suggestion, Professor Salys, as well as Professor Emeritus Allison Blakely of Boston University (European and Comparative History), contributed a previously published article and the foreword, respectively, to this edition of *Chronicle*.

In 2014, following Mr. Patterson's stroke, he could no longer use a computer. His handwriting has deteriorated as to be almost unreadable. Now, he cannot even read his own writing—one of the worst things that can happen to a writer. Fortunately, he told me about his longtime friend Tatiana "Tanya" Boian. Tanya sent me transcripts of her talks with him, which proved an enormous help in writing the photo captions for this book.

As for the translation of one of Mr. Patterson's poems, which appears at the start of *Chronicle*, Professor Razor identified a gifted poet, Andryusha Kuznetsov, who is also a translator of Russian and Yiddish. This scholar and child of Soviet immigrants fleshed out Mr. Patterson's raw emotions in sharp, moving detail, propelling the narrative from page one.

Additionally, I located editor and author Cheryl Ross, whose paternal family of African background, like Mr. Patterson's, hails from Nelson County, Virginia. Like me, she expressed a great fascination with the topic of black Americans seeking full personhood in the Soviet Union and in Mr. Patterson's story. So with that, she signed on to the book.

The topper to bring this project full circle: Anna Lawton of New Academia Publishing, a professor of Russian literature and film studies and a frequent visitor to Moscow, knew about Mr. Patterson and *Circus*. She offered to publish the volume which you hold in your hands.

When Mr. Patterson was a boy, he met Edgar Owens, an African-American member of the Communist Party in America who lived in Russia. Owens gave Mr. Patterson some advice. "I have remembered this for the rest of my life," my friend says.

" 'Be in the swim, kid,' " Mr. Patterson said Owens told him. " 'To learn to swim, you must learn to lie on the water. Put your face down, and the surface will turn into a pillow for you.' "

Every time I see Mr. Patterson is such a treat. He loves to tell stories about his life, each one more fascinating than the next. His eighty-eight years have been full of sorrow and happiness, but he looks upon each day as a gift. Maybe that's why I instantly connected with him—the first time we met, I felt his deep sadness, but his unflagging winning spirit and the deep strength it took for him to keep it waving pulled at my heart. Now, his friends and I are thrilled that he will finally hold the English edition of *Chronicle* in his hands. He's kept his head above raging waters and is truly in the swim.

Amy Ballard
February 2022

Foreword

James Lloydovich Patterson, born in Moscow on July 17, 1933, has enjoyed a truly charmed life. He was the first son of Vera Aralova, a Russian painter, graphic artist, and fashion designer, and her husband, Lloyd Patterson, who had arrived in Russia the year before James's birth as part of a group of young, adventurous black Americans recruited for a soon-to-be aborted Soviet-propaganda film project. In 1936, James achieved instant national fame as a baby actor in a different film, *Tsirk* [*Circus*]. The Russian public's adoration for "Baby James" paralleled that of American audiences' love for Shirley Temple, his contemporary in the United States. In fact, his national audience was even larger than Temple's and it is not much of an exaggeration to say that everyone in the Soviet Union watched the same movies.

In that era, crowds feted James Patterson as the marshal of parades. He remained a privileged celebrity for much of his life. The magnitude of his success as a child star in just that one movie discouraged him from accepting later film roles. During World War II, as a result of the Soviet government's massive evacuation of European Russia in the face of the 1941 German invasion, he went to primary school in Sverdlovsk, in the Ural Mountains. After the war, James attended naval schools, was eventually commissioned as an officer, and pursued a naval career for several years before resigning to become a full-time poet in the 1960s. In the mid-1950s, he had already begun publishing poems in several of the top literary journals (*Moskva, Ogonyok, Voin, Sovetskii Ukraine*). He then published a number of books of poetry and graduated from the Moscow Literary Institute in 1964. Some of his pieces dealt with Russia's relationship to Africa and with African-American themes, including the Little Rock school integration struggle. In the 1990s, he and his mother moved to Washington, DC, at his mother's bidding, hoping to find a wider market for her art.

The book James Patterson offers here in its first English translation—*Chronicle of the Left Hand*—is essentially his paternal grandmother Margaret Glascoe's memoir, which has also led a charmed life. Profizdat, the All-Union Central Council of Trade Unions publishing house, originally released it in 1937 while Margaret worked briefly as a shock worker in an auto parts factory in Russia; her visit, to be closer to her son, Lloyd, lasted three and a half years. She titled the memoir *Dvoinoe iarmo* [*Double Yoke*], alluding to the double burden of racial and economic oppression her family shared with the majority of black people in the United States under slavery and the similarly repressive Jim Crow system that replaced it. James titled a 1964 Russian edition, published by Molodaia Gvardia under his authorship, *Khronika levoi ruki* [*Chronicle of the Left Hand*]. As will become apparent in reading this work, the symbolism of the left hand reflected more clearly that his grandmother was using the experience of four generations of their family's personal hardships in the United States as an exemplary contrast to the official depiction of life in Soviet Russia.

In her version of the book, Margaret humbly admits that she had never picked up a pen to write before arriving in the Soviet Union; and census records show that growing up in a family of sharecroppers allowed her just a third-grade level of formal education. She asks her readers to accept her stories for their message, as a token of gratitude for Soviet hospitality

affording her better living conditions than the racist regime
at home. Other available evidence also affirms that Margaret had scant literacy in English and none at all in Russian.
Therefore, certainly either Lloyd, who ended his studies in
interior decorating at Hampton Institute for the Soviet adven-
ture, or Soviet editors wrote her manuscript. Nevertheless,
this narrative of her family's experience reveals Margaret as a
gifted storyteller; and, although evidence shows that she and
her ghostwriter—or ghostwriters—embellished some of the
book's accounts to make them even stronger contributions to
Soviet antiracist propaganda, this fact can't be denied: Racist oppression in the United States was so intense that even
an unvarnished, factual narrative about it would have been
heady material for Soviet purposes.

So, this manuscript paid dividends for three generations
of the Patterson family; and for our time, it is a valuable relic
of Soviet culture at the climax of its ideological dream phase
that incongruously included one of the worst famines in Russia's long history of famines and Joseph Stalin's nightmarish
political purges. Although the Patterson family's considerable
body of documents shows little awareness of those events,
Margaret's memoir still provides a rare glimpse into that by-
gone era from the perspective of eyewitness participants who
were Afro-American, Afro-Soviet, and fortunate enough to be
protected by the government for their contributions to its political agenda. This made it very important that Lloyd's, Margaret's, and James's writings toe the Communist Party line.
The content of the book probably helped ensure their safety in
a period when even false whispers might lead to government
agents paying an unwelcome visit. It was also important that
Lloyd be officially called a "propagandist," his professional title while he worked for MOPR [International Organization for Aid to Revolutionary Fighters], an affiliate under the
Communist International. The title provides clear evidence of
his usefulness to the Communist cause.

A quarter of a century later, Lloyd's son James appropriated his grandmother's book as the main substance of the writing sample he presented to the Union of Soviet Writers to qualify for his membership, which entailed considerable professional and financial advantages. His original contributions to his grandmother's memoir are a poem at the start; brief annotative commentary looking back from the early 1960s interjected at selected points; and a conclusion consisting of impressionistic musings on events of the 1960s related to social justice. The audience for this new edition can know with hindsight that the Soviet experiment in popular democracy it sought to support collapsed from the weight of its internal contradictions; and that the similarly idealistic American experiment it challenged is still in progress but likewise remains endangered by its own internal contradictions.*

Allison Blakely
Professor of European and Comparative History, Emeritus
Boston University

* I am indebted to Romy Taylor for sharing documentary evidence supportive of my account on the Pattersons here from her own research in Russian archives, those of Hampton University, and African-American newspapers. My thanks as well to Rimgaila Salys for additional advice on sources.

Chronicle of the Left Hand

Моим предкам
                по отцовской линии
Много бед пришлось перетерпеть.
Местной Салтычихой из Виргинии
Мой далекий прадед
                брошен в печь.

В первые мгновения младенчества,
Вспышкой боли ощутив испуг,
Он уже
                остался искалеченным,
Обожжен огнем
                и однорук.
Время раны той не залечило,
И, по-видимому,
                оттого
Ранняя чахотка подточила
Балагура деда моего.
Родину покинувший,
                отмеченную
Горечью лишений и обид,
Мой левша-отец
                в войну Отечественную
За Страну советскую
                погиб.
Не рассказываю
                сказки я,
Только издавна,
        сдается
                мне,
Левая рука,
        как сталь дамасская,
У меня
        закалена в огне.

My ancestors
                on my paternal line
Had to suffer many blows.
Like Saltychikha of Virginia's crime:*
Into the fireplace she throws
                   my forefather from long ago.

Within the baby's very first days
He feels flashes of pain, fright, and alarm
He remained
              forever maimed,
Scorched by flames
                   and left one-armed.
Time never did heal that wound
And that is why,
           I presume,
My grandfather's lungs became consumed
His laughter cut short all too soon.
My father abandoned his homeland
                  where he had endured
The bitter insult of so many things denied.
My father the lefty
              fought the Great Patriotic War
For the Soviet Fatherland
           my father died.
Perhaps you won't believe
          that what I say is real
But since long ago
              I've felt
                as though
My left hand
          is like Damascus steel
forged only stronger
           amid fire's throes.

—*James Lloydovich Patterson*

* Saltychikha refers to Darya Saltykova, a Russian noblewoman and serf owner during the time of Catherine the Great. Her cruelty caused the death of more than thirty-eight serfs.

Chapter 1

My Great-Grandfather Acquires Land

In my time, we had other concerns ... Such as avoiding be-
ing lynched, and moving north if we could, staying alive,
maintaining our dignity.
—Lorraine Hansberry[1]

I, James Lloydovich Patterson, grandson of Margaret Glascoe, peer
into the past and see the United States of Lynching. Before me plays
out the middle of the nineteenth century, stained by blood. I see
rampant human trafficking and the highest clerical powers sanctify-
ing slavery. Virginia is a land ashamed of its past—one of the first
colonies to legalize the deprivation of liberties and rights of people to
render them equivalent to draft animals. Here, babies born of unions
between the free and enslaved remained slaves!

I see my great-grandfather, the black slave Patrick Hager, sitting
cross-legged in the yard under a chestnut tree chewing on a wad of
tobacco. His gray hair falls over his shoulders. His healthy, gnarled
left hand, long fingers, and creased palm dangle onto the ground.

My paternal grandmother, Margaret, passed down his story.
She told me:

Your great-grandfather Patrick Hager was the bastard son
of the plantation owner. The plantation owner's wife hated baby Patrick. [2] A few days after his birth, she threw him
into flames. Someone rescued him, but his right hand suffered mightily. Only two fingers remained. My pa—your
great-grandfather—started life fighting adversity and battled
it to his very end.

Pa sired seven children. The eldest, Mallisia, tall, with long hair and black eyes, embodied the word "beautiful." To us younger ones, she was like a mother.

Charles, the next oldest, we called "big brother." He stood as tall as Pa, and all of the hard work fell on his shoulders. He cut down trees, hauled firewood, and repaired pipes damaged by windstorms.

I hardly knew my sister Sarah Jean. Out of necessity, Pa sent her off to work for a family when she was very young. I don't recall her ever living with us.

The rest of us were little ones: my brothers Sam and Patrick Jr., my sister Clara, and myself. We lived in a cramped log cabin with a dirt floor. In the corner, an iron rod extended from hooks above a stone hearth. From those hooks, we hung pots and pans and cooked over the fire.

The cabin stood atop a high mountain. Our family and two "white trash" families were the only people who lived there. Our nearest neighbors were the McAlexanders.[3]

I try picturing my grandmother's cabin with a hole cut into the wall in lieu of a window, perched on a mountain overgrown with thistles and bushes accessible only on horseback via a circuitous route.

Thin Johnny McAlexander, called "Johnny Mac" behind his back, would stride down the mountain swinging his arms, hunting squirrels, and collecting ginseng.

Now, the door creaks as Martha Baldwin steps onto the porch carrying a bucket.

Our other neighbor was Martha Baldwin, who lived not even half a mile away.

The Baldwins had five children. Mr. Baldwin was paralyzed, and Mrs. Baldwin kept a garden with the help of three of her children, two of whom were still quite young. Sometimes, our pa would send our brothers Sam and Patrick Jr. over to help her out.

Mallisia—we simply called her "Sister"—didn't spend much time with us. She was always washing, ironing, and cooking, if we had anything to cook; but as soon as she sat down, we'd swarm around her asking her to tell a story. I'd climb onto her lap and she'd tell me about our ma, who died before I was even a year old.[4] Mallisia told us that Ma was married off while still a girl and had her first child at age four-teen. Ma hadn't wanted to marry yet, but her father had a lot of children and had insisted she wed so that he'd have one less mouth to feed. Pa, middle-aged when he wed Ma, was no stranger to fatherhood; he had adult children from his first wife—children who had been born into slavery and lived in another state.

I see two people near a sparse hedge. A thin web of dust swirls around their feet. That's my great-grandfather Patrick Hager and the local plantation owner, Higginbotham.[5] Grandma Margaret told me that Higginbotham had ceded the plot overgrown with woods and thickets to her pa. Under an oral agreement between the two men, my great-grandfather was to work the land, but the first three years' harvest would all go to Higginbotham. Great-grandfather Patrick's entire family worked from dawn to dusk. This all happened before Grandma Margaret was born.[6]

Back before my family members moved to the cabin atop the mountain, before I was even a seed in my mother's bel-ly, they experienced hard, hard labor.[7] Mallisia told me that us Hagers chopped down trees, uprooted tree stumps, and moved rocks and boulders. Higginbotham would sell the logs from the trees our family felled and keep the proceeds.

Then one day, Mallisia said, Pa found a "bee tree" in the mountains. Our family caught the bees. Pa spent many eve-nings setting up hives, but the children didn't get to feast on the honey for long. Pa sold it and in turn bought staples and equipment.

A year passed. Through tremendous effort, Pa, Ma, and the siblings I had yet to join cultivated a small vegetable garden. Even though everyone worked themselves to the bone, beans were the only food they had to eat. But Pa never gave up. Mallisia said that one Sunday, he came home to their shack in an especially good mood and said to Ma, "This year, God willing, I'll be selling part of the harvest. Word has it that we can get a plot in the mountains from the government. And in two years, the children can start going to school."

"Patrick, you know full well that the plantation owners won't allow a school for the blacks around here," Ma timidly replied. "They'll never allow the children to go to school when there's work to be done."

"That's why I have to get my own plot of land. Then I'll have the right to vote."

"It doesn't matter if you own land. They'll never let you vote."

"I'll fight for my rights. We're all equal under the law," Pa shot back.

The way Mallisia told the story, Pa was angry and shouting at Ma because she didn't agree with him. The dream of owning his own land totally obsessed him. In his pursuit of this dream, he was willing to work himself silly, not sparing his children either. He believed in the force of law and the kindness of people. When Ma tried to voice her concerns, he flew into a rage and slammed his fist down on the table. Mallisia said he always pointed to Higginbotham as an example of uprightness.

He'd say, "Higginbotham is a great man. There's no better white man in these parts. He gave me this plot of land, didn't he? Ever since abolition, I've never heard another white man say to a Negro, 'Alright, Patrick, get down to business. I'll help you out—in three years' time, I'll hand this plot of land over to you.' "

Mallisia told me the rest of the sad tale:

In two years, Pa had already cleared a large part of land for farming. Higginbotham didn't live far away, and he'd drop by every week to see how things were going. His two elder children, Walter and Frank, attended school in town, while the three younger children lived on the farm.

After Walter and Frank returned home upon graduating, Higginbotham summoned Pa. His two-storied white house with a wide wraparound porch reached toward the sky in a charming valley not far from the main road. Attached to the house stood sheds, barns, and an icehouse. The house cook had told Pa that her masters lived high off the hog but fed the workers bare pickings; she stole food on the sly because otherwise she'd starve to death. Pa was hesitant about entering the house through the back door, which was what Negroes usually used, and greeted Higginbotham from the gate.

I can see them, how the two men take a seat on a log. I eavesdrop on their conversation.

"Here's the deal, Pat. Next year I'm thinking of giving you horses to help you out, and you'll get a third of the harvest. You don't have the means to work the land, and I'll give you everything you need."

"But, Mr. Higginbotham, you gave your word. You said you'd give me the land in three years. I've cleared a lot of it with my bare hands—you can't deny that. My entire family's been working day and night. I'll clear my debts somehow this year, and next year I expect to generate a small profit. No, it's out of the question. I won't agree to your new offer."

"But, Pat, you see, my boys are done with their schooling and want to start farming. You've got the best land now. I can't hand it over to you until next year."

"True, it is the best; but until I cleared that land, it was nothing but thickets and shrubs."

"Come on now, Pat. I can't do a thing about it. I need that land."

"What about our agreement, Mr. Higginbotham?"

"I'm not obliged to honor it."

Pa returned home completely shattered, as if broken. The

land into which he'd poured so much sweat and tears was slipping out of his hands, and with it, his dream of escaping poverty and getting back on his feet. His eyes empty, he gazed upon his shack and the children running around the yard. Ma glanced at him fearfully, afraid to ask about what the plantation owner had said.

When it came to selling his honey, Pa still had high hopes. He figured that he could earn about three hundred dollars from it. He spent every free minute tending to the bees. His children weren't allowed near the hives; but the honey didn't bring him any luck either.

One Sunday, Pa asked Higginbotham for a horse to take the family to the Negro church. The family got back late and went straight to bed. The next morning, Pa saw that the hives were ruined and the honey had been stolen. Nearby, he found a hat that belonged to Higginbotham's son Walter.

An unbelievable anger gripped Pa. He grabbed the ancient gun over the family's door, roused his oldest son from the sofa, and the two of them began to head over to the Higginbothams' place. Ma tried to stop them from leaving, but Pa shoved her out of the way. She'd never seen him so enraged.

The sun was high in the sky by the time Pa and Charles returned home. Pa was muttering under his breath, "No good thieves. They'll pay me. The law is on my side!" Over breakfast, he said to Ma, "They did this to drive me off the land, but I won't leave until I'm done with my three years. Then this land will be mine. I'll no longer work for the master, and I won't let my children work for him either."

The family was out working in the field when the sheriff came by. "You'll pay for what you did, you smelly nigger," he said.

"But we've already settled matters," said Pa. "Mr. Higginbotham said he'd pay me for the honey his sons stole."

"Yes, that's right, but we have laws, and you broke one of them. What makes you think you can show up at a white man's home with a gun? Now get your things together and come with me!"

His head down, Pa stood in front of the sheriff. Then he called our brother Charles over, put his hands on Charles's shoulders, and said, "Son, you're the man here now. You have to look after your ma and your sisters. Go see Kimble Anderson and tell him what went down here."

Ma said nothing as the sheriff led Pa away. She just looked at him through her watery tears. Pa had never said a word about what transpired at Higginbotham's plantation, but Charles soon told her about it.

Earlier, when they got to Higginbotham's, Charles told Ma, his sons were sleeping. Charles had knocked on the window, and one of the sons, Frank, had walked onto the porch. Pa showed him the hat and said, "Frank, isn't this Walter's hat?"

Just then, Walter stepped outside. Still not fully awake, he said, "Yes, that's my hat. How come you have it?"

"Alright," Pa said. "You stole my honey, and I want you to pay for it."

"What are you saying, old man?" Walter shouted. "Are you out of your mind? Somebody else probably dropped my hat there."

Pa raised the rifle in a resolute manner. "Are you going to pay me? Don't make me mad now!"

Just then, Higginbotham, clearly upset, strode across the porch. "Yes, of course we'll pay! Enough. I won't allow you to fool around with me and mine!"

With that, Pa carefully backed out of the yard, rifle still raised. Charles trailed after him, glancing wide-eyed at Higginbotham, whose face was red with rage.

Pa's courage, however, had not served him well. Now he was in jail, facing a harsh punishment.

Chapter 2

Blacklisted

"Master Stevens got wind that Pa was trying to organize blacks and said that he wouldn't allow a rebel at his place."[8]

Ma left the young ones in Charles's care, and she went to Kimble Anderson, a kind, older man who ran a shop in a nearby settlement, about ten miles from Higginbotham's estate. Although Anderson was white, he'd always treated Pa well. On this day, he listened attentively to Ma's account of events. Then he sat back and mulled things over.

Finally, Anderson said, "It looks bad, Sarah, bad. I told Patrick over and over again not to trust Higginbotham too much. All rich people are the same. I'll go to town and see what I can do for your husband."

Not long after Ma returned from seeing Anderson, Higginbotham showed up at the shack. He was unusually nice and spoke eloquently, trying to soften his typically harsh tone.

"See, Sarah," he said, "I don't wish you any harm. Yes, your man threatened me with a rifle, but I'm not angry with him. I'm a good man. I don't want to hurt you. But, of course, after what's happened, I can't allow you to stay here. Convince your husband to get off my land and I'll drop the case against him. Do you know what kind of trouble he's in? They'll send him off to work on a chain gang. What'll happen to your family then?"

Mother sat with her head lowered as she cried silently. What choice did she have? She promised Higginbotham that she'd do her best to talk Pa into leaving.

One week later, Pa was back home, having been released on bail while awaiting trial. Kimble Anderson had posted the bail.

Being in jail had been hard on Pa, but his fighting spirit soared. "The law is on my side!" he said. "I'm staying on this land until I get what I'm owed for clearing it. I have the right to protect what's mine from thieves. The court has to agree. I'll teach that Higginbotham and his thieving sons a lesson."

Mother dared not say a word. But Pa's stubbornness and unshakable resolve frightened her. She knew better than Pa that a poor Negro didn't have a chance in court against a wealthy plantation owner.

At the trial, the judge asked, "Did you go to the residence of Mr. Higginbotham, who provided you with land at no charge, with a gun?"

"What do you mean 'at no charge'? I cleared a huge plot of that land for him. He sold the lumber from one portion of the woods for more than five hundred dollars. Mr. Higginbotham's sons stole my honey, and I went to his house to ensure I got paid for what it was worth."

"What proof do you have that Mr. Higginbotham's sons stole your honey?"

"I found one of their hats in the yard."

"Humph! Well, here's the thing, Patrick. Mr. Higginbotham's sons were just messing with you, and Mr. Higginbotham doesn't want to see you put in jail. I know you're a hard worker, so I'm giving you a month to find another place. In that time, you have to leave Mr. Higginbotham's land."

"What about my harvest?"

"What? You're not satisfied with that? Even after showing up at a white man's house bearing arms?"

"What about my honey? My two years of hard work?"

"Mr. Higginbotham's sons are minors. They can't be charged under the law," the judge said.

Just like that, the law drove Pa off the land that he'd watered with his sweat. At the trial, another plantation owner, this one by the name of Mr. Boyd, threw out a lifeline to Pa, who had a reputation as an excellent worker. Mr. Boyd offered Pa employment and a place to live, to which Pa agreed.

Soon, Pa was harnessing his bull to a cart, loading his wretched belongings on it, and setting off with our family in search of happiness. He left behind him a rich harvest and the remnants of his shattered dreams.

Our family moved into an old, unoccupied, rundown cabin that listed to one side as it clung to what the locals called Snake Hill. Thick overgrowth and weeds teeming with snakes surrounded the dejected cabin set amidst an area with no roads or other paths. Mallisia recalled how Pa's cart creaked and swayed as it slowly plowed through the bushes and brambles and how on the very first night in the cabin, Pa killed two moccasins.

At the foot of the hill, not far from the "new" place, a spring fought its way through the weeds. There had been no way to get to the cabin until Charles had cut a narrow path through. Afterward, all day long, Ma and Pa had struggled to make the cabin livable. To drive away the snakes, they set rags on fire and scattered them about the yard.

Mr. Boyd, Pa's new employer, was a wealthy plantation owner, even richer than Higginbotham. He lived on an impressive estate. His kitchen was housed in a cabin separate from the house. Several maids served the household, and fine horses and carriages filled the stable.

Pa worked a full year as a farmhand for Mr. Boyd for next to nothing. The rest of the family worked for him too. Ma earned $1.50 a month by washing clothes. Mr. Boyd had six children and two white farmhands, so Ma was busy all day long. She wasn't paid in money. They paid her with produce.

Charles helped Pa in the field, and Mallisia, who was only eight years old, took care of the master's children. She not only tended after the toddlers, she worked around the house. She fetched water from the spring and washed the floors and diapers. The Boyds fed her and gave her some milk for the younger ones.

Though our family had Mr. Boyd to thank for employment, the truth is that if it had not been for Kimble Anderson, the man who bailed Pa out of jail, the family would probably have starved. Pa often borrowed money from him. Anderson wasn't a rich man, but he was always willing to help Pa.[9]

After the crops were harvested, Mr. Boyd allotted a small plot to Pa and gave him a horse. Pa was supposed to raise crops on the allotment and give Mr. Boyd two-thirds of the proceeds. He did, and that's how Pa became a sharecropper. Though he wanted to be an independent landowner, here he was working under the same conditions he had with Higginbotham.

Every Sunday, Pa attended church. He wasn't religious, but at the service, he could meet up and talk with other black people. Once, he brought the entire family to church. A lot of people were gathered outside. The women were dressed in their finest garb. Red bows, white bibs, and soft hats made up the scene. Some rode in on mules, others on horses, and others on bulls. Everyone brought food.

The preacher strode up to the pulpit and spoke so loudly and passionately that you couldn't make anything out. He'd sputter and slam his fist on the Bible. The older men and women, his parishioners, would say, "Amen! Alleluia! Glory be to God." Then some woman would dash out into the middle of the aisle, clapping her hands and jumping high. She'd knock off someone's hat and step on people's feet, shouting, "Glory be! Praise the Lord!" A man would step forward to pick her up, and she'd sway back and forth.

For the youngsters, this was all new, interesting.

Mallisia asked Ma, "Why are they doing that, Mama?"

"They're rejoicing," Ma calmly said.

"What for? Do they really have enough to eat? Don't they have to work?"

Ma cut Mallisia off. "Hush, child! Don't talk like that!"

By the time everyone filed out of the church, the tables under the trees were already set up. After everyone finished eating, Pa stood and addressed the crowd.

He said, "I know it's not proper to talk about work on a day like this, but we don't get together very often. As is written in the Bible, if an ox falls into the swamp, then you must pull it out. It seems to me that we here are facing adversity. Bill Voguin has six children, yet his master took the whole crop for himself and he's pushing Bill out. It's all because Bill wants his boys to go to school."

Pa continued, "Bill bought a piglet last spring, as you're all aware. His master suggested he have the pig feed with his lot. Now, he won't let Bill have the pig back and wants half the proceeds as payment for feed."

Everyone was silent, then someone said, "What can we do to help Bill? We're all struggling with the harvest. You know full well, Pat, that whenever we Negroes band together, the white landowners get upset with us and—"

Pa cut him off. "I wasn't saying that we could help Bill with his material needs. What I'd like to see are all twenty-four of us black-skinned laborers and sharecroppers unite, work out some rules. These rules would be binding on all of us. Whenever an owner steals from the crop yield due to a good worker, no one else should work for that owner. If we all hold fast to this rule, we'll put a stop to this kind of treatment by the white man."

Not many that day agreed with Pa. The majority assumed that his proposal spelled even more trouble for them.

"What you're suggesting won't do us any good," one man said. "You'll just get us all lynched."

So, Pa's attempt to unite the farmhands and sharecroppers went nowhere. Not long after this, something so bad happened to a sharecropper named Jim Bush that everyone else was too cowed to stand by Pa at all.

Bush worked as a sharecropper for a plantation owner named Jones. He had labored for three years on Jones's land, uprooting stumps, clearing brush, and hauling off rocks. His family lived from hand to mouth, suffering incredible deprivation.

His eldest son worked on another plantation. The lad worked like an ox and gave everything he earned to his father. So, in year four of working for Jones, Jim Bush bought himself a horse and a cow. This was his first step toward independence.

The plantation owner Jones didn't like this one bit. Once a sharecropper acquired a horse or stock, he got half of the yield, not just a third. Jones was also not at all pleased that Bush, his sharecropper, was "moving up" in the world. He started looking for any excuse to get rid of him.

Bush's second eldest son was twelve years old and often played with Jones's son, who was the same age. One day, the two boys got into a fight. Jones was sitting on his porch when he heard the ruckus. He went to check it out and found his son straddling his playmate and giving him a drubbing. The black workers harvesting apples were trying to separate the two, but Jones wouldn't let them.

"Don't interfere," he said. "Let them fight."

Bush's son was bleeding. His eyes were so black and blue that they were almost closed. Somehow, however, he managed to use his legs like scissors and flip the plantation owner Jones's son onto his back. Before Jones could stop him, he slugged his son over and over.

That's when Jones laid into Bush's son. He grabbed him, hauled him up, and slammed his fist into him. Then he let him drop onto the ground, leaving the child's face bloodied.

Jones wasn't through. He stomped on the child with his boot, kicking him in the chest and stomach until he fell into unconsciousness. Then Jones calmly walked back to his porch and sat down.

Someone brought Bush's son some water and tried to revive him, but to no avail. They sent for Bush, who was working in the field, and called in a doctor.

Bush ran to the scene, breathless, arriving ashen-faced and filled with despair. In a low voice, he asked the doctor, who had made it there before him, "Will he survive?"

"I'm sorry, Bush," the doctor said, "but I have to tell you that your son won't live more than two days. His kidneys are shot. There's nothing I can do."

For two days, the young man remained unconscious as his father stayed by his side. After he died, Bush grabbed his shotgun and visited Jones. Jones was, to all appearances, completely calm. Like usual, he sat smoking on his porch.

"Mister Jones," Bush said, "get your gun. One of us is following my son on his journey today."

"Alright," Jones replied. He motioned as if about to go inside for a gun, but then he suddenly drew his revolver and fired at Bush. The bullet pierced Bush's hat. Bush then discharged everything he had into Jones's abdomen. After that, Bush went to the sheriff and turned himself in.

The townspeople responded harshly to what went down. Mobs of men up to no good marched about the streets raucously threatening blacks. They grabbed one young black man near a store and shouted, "Here's a nigger! Let us have some fun!" Then they beat him up. The son of a white sharecropper named Gansey, who worked for Mr. Boyd, tried to intervene. They beat him up too, saying, "Don't stand up for no nigger!"

This triggered more savagery. The crazed mob burst into the jail, and nobody tried to stop them when they pulled Bush out of his cell. They hanged him two miles outside of town with a sign on his chest: "A warning to all niggers who show disrespect to their masters."

Next, the mob moved on to Bush's house. At that time, Bush's wife was pregnant. She rushed out the back door to escape the mob and tumbled down a steep embankment. She perished mere days after her son and husband, leaving four children and a grown son. This son was afraid to return home. They went on the hunt for him.

Next, a wave of terror against blacks ensued. Mr. Gansey's son, who the mob had attacked, lay in bed for a week. Mr. Gansey told Pa that he'd provide the Negroes weapons and ammunition if they wanted to band together.

Pa tried to talk about it with blacks who worked on Mr. Boyd's land. They were all so frightened though that they turned a deaf ear.

Then Pa quit working for Mr. Boyd and started working for another plantation owner by the name of Stevens. Stevens's estate sat on the other side of the mountain, not far from the Negro school.

Thomas, another black sharecropper working for Stevens, had six children. Three of them attended school. Stevens told Thomas not to let his children go to school during the workday, and Tom curtly responded, "When isn't there work to be done, Mr. Stevens? If they don't go to school during the workday, they won't go to school at all. Is that what you want?"

An argument erupted.

Stevens said that he'd teach that nigger a lesson for disrespecting a white man.

That evening, Pa and a few other blacks, as well as several other sharecroppers who worked for Stevens, gathered at Tom's place and stayed the night there to protect him. They expected a mob to descend on his home.

But nothing happened. Stevens and his cohorts apparently figured out that they'd face opposition were they to make a show. The upshot was, however, that Pa again had to move on. Stevens got wind that Pa was trying to organize blacks and said he wouldn't stand for an uppity nigger on his land.

It was autumn, and my father traveled from one place to another trying to find employment. Everywhere he went, he heard the same thing: "We don't need no Negro troublemakers."

That's how my great-grandfather Patrick Hager was blacklisted. So, he decided to move to the mountains. There, deep in the woods, he dug holes in the ground, put posts in them, and made a thatch cabin.

This was the new domicile of the Hager family. Grandma Margaret said that inside they had thatch spread over dirt instead of a wooden floor. They had no furniture; nothing even to sit on ... Charles cut down a tree in the forest and made blocks that served as seats. Then he took a log he'd felled, used an ax to fashion a board, burned holes in it, and inserted legs. The result was a bench for the head of the family. It always stood by the hearth. Pa would sit on it staring into the fire, chewing tobacco. In that cabin at the top of a mountain, Sarah Hager would give birth to her last child—my grandmother Margaret.

Chapter 3

On His Own Land

"The earth could not feed two ..."[10]

After many years of struggle and hardship, Pa's cherished dream had come true. The state awarded him a few acres of uncultivated land on the top of the mountain where our new cabin stood.

Pa's joy knew no bounds. He seemed younger and began to develop the site with gusto.

As soon as my family moved in, my mother began cleaning houses for other people, although she was pregnant with me. After my birth, she continued working.[11] She had to because Pa had yet to earn a living from working the land. All he could do was pay taxes. Ma developed consumption from working so hard and died while I was very young.

My brother Charles worked as a farmhand for a plantation owner. Sometimes, he'd come home and stay with us for a while. Pa and the other children worked the land.

Our neighbor Mrs. Baldwin would often come by to help Mallisia. This kind woman would clean up around the place and bathe us. Whenever we needed help and Pa wasn't around, we'd go to her. Though she was white, we all loved her dearly.

At some point, Mallisia left us. She started working as a domestic for a doctor. Losing Mallisia was like losing Ma again. Now, our second oldest brother, Sam, had to step in as a mother figure.

Sam made us dinner and sewed clothes. He'd make our shifts out of flower sacks. Often, we went about almost stark naked. The good Mrs. Baldwin didn't have anything either, so she had nothing to share with us.

Charles came back home after serving his year as a farmhand and brought with him a cow. So, now we had milk and corn cakes to eat.

One evening, all of us except Mallisia gathered at home while Pa sat, as usual, on his bench by the hearth. Charles turned to him and said, "Pa, tell us about yourself. You've lived such a hard life. I can't imagine how you endured slavery. I wish I was like you!"

"You see, son of mine, slavery wasn't so bad for me. Our master, the plantation owner, was my father. He didn't let anyone beat me, nor was I sold off."

"Is that why you have such fair skin? Did you love your father?"

"No, I hated him. My mother had a family—a husband and children. But the master fancied her and sold her husband to another plantation owner. He sold her children too, for next to nothing. One of her sons, Phil, loved his mama so much that he didn't want to go. He said that he'd do whatever they told him to do if only he could stay by his ma's side. So, he lived on the Anderson's estate until the master's death. I'll tell you about Phil. You'll see what kind of a person he was," Pa said as he stared into the fire. "Phil loved a girl who lived on a neighboring plantation. He wanted to marry her. However, because he was a slave he had to get the master's approval. Anderson was dead by then, so Phil approached his wife. Mrs. Anderson was a Southerner to the core, so she was cruel. Because of Ma, she was especially harsh to our family.

"Phil was a healthy young guy. They called him a 'thoroughbred' as if he were a cow or a horse. The mistress of the plantation didn't want to lose him, so she said, 'Choose a bride from one of our girls. I'm not letting you leave here, and henceforward, I forbid you to meet up with that girl you want to marry. If you do, I'll have you flogged.'

"But Phil couldn't keep away from the girl. He was crazy about her. Someone reported him to the mistress. She summoned the overseer to have Phil whipped as she watched.

"The overseer snarled at Phil, 'Okay, nigger, take off that shirt!'

"They stood near the porch where the mistress sat. Phil was desperate. He turned to Mrs. Anderson and said, 'I've always obeyed you. The master would never lay a hand on me, nor would he allow others to do so. Now I'm thirty-two years old. The shame will kill me if you flog me.'

"Still the overseer roared, 'Listen to me, nigger, get that shirt off!' He was repulsive.

"The long whip he clutched writhed on the ground like a snake. He swung it and lashed Phil with all his might. The whip encircled his torso, and the overseer dragged Phil toward him. Then, Phil heard a rustling in the grass nearby. Somebody had tossed a sickle into the middle of the yard. Phil grabbed it and swiftly slashed open the overseer's abdomen. Then he took off running. They unleashed the bloodhounds and went looking for him, but he got away."

"So your last name is Anderson, not Hager?" Charles asked.

"Hager was my mother's family name."

"So that's why Kimble Anderson was so good to us. He's your cousin, right?"

"No, he's my half-brother—my father's son. As the master aged, he often ailed, and once he took me into the woods with him and had a long talk with me. He said that he loved my mother, wanted to set her free and make our life easier. Most of all, he wanted me to think well of him after he died.

"He said to me, 'I've always cared about you. You know that, don't you?'

"At first, I didn't respond. For a slave, he treated me well, but I was his son. In my opinion, what he did for me wasn't enough considering I was his son. I was a slave, and his children were my masters. That's what I told him. There was no way to bridge the space between us. He was my master before and still was my master at that time, and I was his slave.

"When he died, I was there when they read his will. He left me a part of the plantation and ordered that I be set free; but I wasn't given freedom, nor was I given a portion of the estate.

"So, I secured my own freedom. I joined the Yankees when the Civil War broke out, and after the war ended I came back to the plantation as a free man."

Grandma Margaret!

When I was a little boy, you'd rock me in your arms and sing songs to me like Mahalia Jackson in a soulful voice. One song you sang was about John Brown.

John Brown's body lies amoldering in the grave,
John Brown's body lies amoldering in the grave,
John Brown's body lies amoldering in the grave,
But his soul goes marching on.

When I hear this name, I start feeling like it was me, and not my great-grandfather Patrick Hager, who marched into battle with a much-lauded Northern regiment. That it was me, lying there bleeding, that I am the one who fought for my freedom. But the victory I fought for bore bitter fruit.

Trouble was still our lot. Once, Pa was absentmindedly smoking in the shed and a spark from his pipe set fire to the entire crop of tobacco laid out to dry there. We faced hardships that year because of that. Pa had to sell the cow to pay off the debts. Once again, our family only had beans to eat.

Then something awful happened to Sam. Pa sent him to the mill to get the corn ground into cornmeal. This was a traditional mill powered by water. No guardrails surrounded the huge millstones. Sam was playing around them as they ground the meal. Somehow, his hand got caught under the stones and his fingers were crushed. The miller used a knife to cut off the fingers, which were dangling from their tendons. He smeared the stubs of Sam's hand with beef lard and sent him home. Nobody called the doctor, knowing that Pa couldn't pay him. The hand soon healed; but not long after that, Sam developed an abscess on his leg.

Now, Sam was always with me. He could no longer run around climbing trees and such with the other kids. He used to make me dolls out of cornstalks and pine cones, and we'd make mud pies that we'd dry in the sun. Sam loved me very much, as I did him. Now that his leg was sore, he couldn't care for me as much.

Soon after that, we would lose another friend. Reluctantly, Mrs. Baldwin would move away. Ironically, this would be our family's doing, even though nobody loved her more in those parts than we did.

Many of the plantation people looked at her askance for her relationship with us. One such neighbor was unpleasant, angry Johnny McAlexander, who derived satisfaction from being quarrelsome.

Once, my brother Pat Jr. cut his hand with a knife. His screams prompted Mrs. Baldwin to run over to help. As she was tending to him, Johnny Mac came by.

"There she is," he said with a mean smile. "That's why you weren't home. You might as well be Pat Hager's mistress. I heard the rumors but didn't believe them."

Mrs. Baldwin blushed and said angrily, "Johnny Mac, shut your filthy mouth! Patrick helps me out just as I do him. He's always been there to lend me a hand ever since I was left to fend for myself with the children. But you, have you ever helped me?"

"If I'd known you'd be as sweet to me as you are to Pat, I just might have helped out," Johnny Mac said, laughing.

Just then, Pa came running in from the field. Someone had told him something happened to his son. Johnny Mac didn't wait around to hear what Mrs. Baldwin had to say to Pa about him, and he left. From there, he went around to several neighbors feigning shock at the "fact" that Martha Baldwin was now Pat Hager's mistress.

The next day, Kimble Anderson warned Pa that a raid on his cabin was planned for that night. Pa headed for the neighbor in the mountains, returning with weapons, and he had us sleep in the barn. As soon as he heard a twig snapping or shrubs rustling in the dark, Pa fired. If attackers had been approaching, they were loath to draw any nearer. Pa had two guns and plenty of bullets, and everybody knew it.

But a band of thugs visited Mrs. Baldwin in the night and told her she'd better clear out in two days. Sadly, she didn't have what it took to handle threats like that. She gathered her children and left the next day. As we said goodbye, we all shed bitter tears.

Now, the only friend we had left was our dog, Guard. Guard was old, but he was great at spotting snakes. Our family had acquired him long before my birth. When I was just a baby, Ma would leave me in his care. Whenever I wanted to take a nap, Guard would check out the bushes around me, making sure there weren't any snakes, and he'd drag me by the shirt to a good spot and lay down beside me. I'd sleep on his paws, and he'd keep everyone and everything away.

Sometimes, local boys would try to lure him away with bread. He'd gobble up the food but wouldn't stray from my side. Whenever we searched for berries in the woods, he'd go in first. Occasionally, he'd suffer a snakebite. Pa would treat him with some kind of herb. Guard would retreat to the bushes and lie there with feverish eyes and a swollen head until he recovered.

We children would wander all over the mountains with Guard as we looked for eagle and kite nests on treetops and wreaked havoc with hornets' nests. The hornets would go crazy trying to defend their dwellings. They'd fly at us, aiming for the eye. Just the same, we loved destroying their nests. If a hornet successfully stung one of us in the brow, the eye would practically swell shut.

It was a hard winter that year, and Pa barely managed to feed us. Sam was always sick with something, but Pa still couldn't bring in the doctor because he had no means to pay him.

One day, the large, painful boil on Sam's leg prompted him to sharpen a knife and to ask me to pierce the abscess. I was terribly frightened, but I loved Sam and wanted to help him. He turned his head, his eyes screwed shut, and I stabbed him in the leg. The boil burst, and pus and blood oozed out. It hurt so badly that Sam fainted. Eventually, he came to with my help, but he remained in pain.

When Pa got back, he was upset, seeing what we'd done. He worried that Sam might get blood poisoning; but Sam started to get better. In fact, before long he was helping Pa around the place. Pa wasn't as strong as he used to be. His broad, muscular shoulders started slumping. Life was more and more trying. The land wasn't generating a profit yet, but he still had to make payments on it, although he was promised it for next to nothing.

Meanwhile, Charles and Mallisia didn't have much to give Pa from what they earned. Their pay was paltry. Sarah Jean worked as a housemaid for room and board. She didn't get paid at all.

It had been a long time since we'd purchased clothes. For us girls, this was especially tough. If the dress tore in the front, we would put it on backward and keep on wearing it. If strangers dropped by, we'd back up to the door and then run outside. As for Pa, he always wore the same shirt.

I remember Pa's long, thin yellow legs. Once, when we went to the mill, someone gave him some old trousers. We teased him, calling him "Mill Pants." He disliked that, so he took off the trousers, put on his old pants, and gave the trousers away.

After gathering the crops, we started readying the land for next year's planting. Pa would do the plowing while we all helped around the house. My brothers would stock up on firewood for the winter. Clara and I would pull weeds.

Pa put up a new fence around the field, but the wind deposited a lot of weeds there. So, one cold evening, we set about clearing the field. To keep us warm, Sam built a fire on the stump. Lacking Sam's experience, I built a fire right on the ground. The flames quickly spread through the dry grass to the weeds by the fence and seemed to consume the entire mountain. People poured in from all over to try to put the fire out. Pa's new fence burned to the ground. For two days, the fire raged until finally it died.

After this, Pa lost hope. He'd worked so long and so hard, with pathetic results. He told Charles that he was thinking that going away somewhere might be best; his luck might change in a new place. Charles agreed.

"You know, Pa, I want to go to West Virginia this year. I can work in a mine there. I can make some money and send for you. We'll buy ourselves a little house, and the kids can go to school."

"That'd be very nice, son, but I can't leave this place until the term is up; otherwise, the work I put into it this year will be lost. But when I get what I'm supposed to, we'll head west."

Again, Sam fell ill. His leg was very swollen. He lay in bed and stayed there. Nobody looked after him. Sometimes, I'd run in from the field to give him some water, and that's it.

One day, we returned home late from the field. Exhausted, I lay down next to Sam. I thought he was sleeping, so I gently pressed my face to his. It was as cold as ice. Sam was dead!

The whole family attended Sam's funeral. After the burial, we went back to the cabin and Pa talked about the future with us.

Chapter 4

A New Era in Life

"I would awake at five in the morning and wouldn't go to bed before midnight. There was no end to the work ..."[12]

Bad luck and troubles broke Pa. He'd poured his entire life into land, a staggeringly disappointing exercise. Hunger regularly visited our cabin. We children had to work. We couldn't go to school.

Pa no longer had the strength to keep up the fight. He told us that he decided to send me to Washington, DC, to Mrs. Signora Hunter, who had no children of her own.[13] Pa didn't know her well at all, but she'd written that she could take in one of his girls and raise her. Meanwhile, he said, he'd send my sister Clara to live with one of our kin.

"She'll be able to attend school there," he said. "And when I'm done paying off this land, we can all live together again. Until then, Patrick and I will maintain this place."

They bought me a dress, shoes, and a hat to prepare to send me off to Mrs. Hunter's.

Clara wasn't happy that I got to go to the city while she stayed behind. When I was just about all packed up and ready to leave, she ran off. I went to look for her out back, but she ran off again as soon as she saw me.

We hadn't received any education. We had learned from the world around us: the birds, the bees, ants, snakes, and beetles. The sun in the sky was how we told time. We didn't know about things like clocks. We knew the season by bird-song, just as we knew much more from nature.

But we were totally ignorant about people, including their customs and norms.

Pa and Patrick accompanied me as I set off on my first journey with a bundle of my belongings on my back. We walked all day and spent the night at the house of an old black man that Pa knew. The next morning, I bade my brother farewell. He had to get back home. I looked back at him over and over, and he kept looking back at me.

Throughout the next day, Pa and I walked, and finally, toward evening, we could hear the whistle of the steam engine wafting our way. We were nearing the train station.

In those days, the trains weren't segregated. Whites and blacks sat together. Pa sat me down in one car and asked the conductor to look after me on the journey, then he left the train. I sat by the window and looked out at my father. He was very moved, but he tried not to show it. I stared at him until I could no longer see him.

Sadness and fear filled me. This would be my first time away from my family. I was nine years old.

At the Alma Station, a black woman entered the car and sat down next to me. [14] Pa forgot to provide me food for the trip, and this woman, beautiful, kind, and inquisitive, shared her breakfast. She asked me questions about myself and my journey. Soon, I felt brave enough to answer her and tell her some of my story.

We chatted until we got to her stop, Alexandria Station.

"Alexandria! Alexandria!" the conductor shouted as he walked by.

I started looking around for Johnny McAlexander but didn't see him.

"Where is he?" I asked the nice lady.

"Who?"

"Mr. Johnny McAlexander."

"Who's that? Is he someone you know?"

"Yes."

The woman laughed.

"The conductor isn't calling anybody. That's just the name of the town. I have to leave you now."

She picked up her things and headed for the exit. I ran after her.

"No, no. Sit down, girl," the nice lady said. "This isn't your stop."

But I kept heading toward the exit. A white woman said to the black woman, "Don't worry, I'll look after the girl. I'm going all the way to Washington." Then the white woman walked up and joined me.

I'd felt immediately at ease with the black woman, but this new woman, though she had a gentle smile, inspired my usual shyness. I shrunk into myself and stared down at my hands. She was so gentle and kind, however, that I suddenly remembered Mrs. Baldwin, our neighbor.

Finally, in Washington, I found myself alone in the station after my second companion departed. The conductor led me to the luggage section and told me to wait there for the next train. It was to take me to Benning Station, not far from DC.

Benning turned out to be a small place with a dirty street running through it.[15] On this street sat a post office, the butcher and grocer, and a drugstore.

Mrs. Hunter's house stood at the end of the street, on the very edge of the woods. It boasted six large rooms and a semisubterranean basement that housed a tavern. A wide porch graced the front of the house. It put me in mind of a zoo.

On the porch, Mr. Hunter was moving things around—living "things." I'm talking owls, eagles, monkeys, squirrels, rabbits, white rats, and snakes, all in cages.

The porch featured tables and chairs for guests, and a living room adjoined it. At the end of a long corridor, I would soon discover, Mrs. Hunter had a workshop for her sewing business. Eight girls worked there.

When I walked onto the porch and knocked on the door the first time, a chorus of dogs barked. Mr. Hunter had around eighteen of them. They scared me, and I thought about home for the first time that entire trip. Mrs. Signora Hunter broke my reverie when she herself responded to my knock. The first words I heard from this small, lively woman with an evil face and sharp eyes were, "I didn't know she'd be so little! And what, is she dumb? It'll be a while before she's able to work."

Just like that, a new era in my life began. Mrs. Hunter didn't need a little girl at all. She wanted a housemaid to do all of the chores. She'd written to Pa hoping that he'd send one of his girls. She'd figured that if she said she'd adopt the girl and let her attend school, he'd be happy to oblige.

As for Mr. Hunter, he was a tall, well-built fellow with a reputation as a businessman. He drank excessively and always had bleary eyes. The Hunters were very close. Mr. Hunter made money from his wheeling and dealing, while Mrs. Hunter exploited the girls. She squeezed everything she could out of people.

The Hunter house and grounds spanned several acres. Numerous household servants worked there. The couple tasked me with washing dishes, making beds, sweeping and mopping floors, and feeding the pigs, dogs, and chickens. I worked from dawn until well into the night. I would awake at five in the morning and wouldn't go to bed before midnight. There was no end to the work. I still have scars on my head from a beating I endured there; I fell asleep in the woods from sheer exhaustion while gathering leaves for the hog pen, and for that, they punished me.

My first winter with the Hunters, I attended school for four months. Schooling wasn't compulsory. Mrs. Hunter took advantage of this by gradually taking me out of school. I was doing washing and ironing instead. Mrs. Hunter taught me how to sew, and she made sure that I could mop floors, cook, and pick up around the place too. Mr. Hunter wore starched shirtfronts. I had to ensure that they didn't have a single wrinkle.

The neighbors were outraged by how hard I worked instead of going to school. They filed a complaint against the Hunters, but Mr. Hunter had a lot of connections and the case was decided in his favor.

The country was about to elect a new president when Pa came to visit me. He stayed at the Hunters for a week. It was like a real holiday. Mrs. Hunter hired a girl to do all the housework in my place. She said to me, "Maggie, dear, I want you to have a break while your pa is here. Call me 'Aunt Signora' [I'd been calling her Mrs. Hunter]. This girl will do all the dirty work. And that song that I taught you to play on the piano—you have to play it for your father. I'm going to keep teaching you music."

These were happy days. I usually got up before everyone else. But now "Aunt Signora" said to me, "Sleep in. I'll wake you up myself." I never ate with the Hunters at the same table because I always had to serve them; but now we dined together.

Mrs. Hunter was so bent on entertaining Pa that he had no time to talk to me. Every day, he and Mr. Hunter would go somewhere and get back late at night.

Pa appeared visibly younger. Everyone seemed to be in love with him. When he didn't go out, the neighbors would drop by for a visit, so even then I couldn't talk to him. Pa was happy to converse with everyone, even though he didn't know them; they'd invite him over and he'd go. If we ended up alone for even a minute, "Aunt Signora" would swoop into the room. So, I couldn't tell Pa what my life was like with her and her husband.

Another reason forced me to keep my mouth shut too.

I feared that Mrs. Hunter would kill me if she ever suspected I complained to Pa. Once, when Mr. Hunter was gone, she had beat me so badly that my whole body had been covered in bruises. The next day, Mr. Hunter learned about this from a neighbor.

He called me over and asked if it was true that "Auntie" had beat me. I kept silent, too scared to tell him what had happened. Then he unbuttoned my dress and saw the bruises on my back. A big scene followed; Mr. Hunter yelled and yelled at "Aunt Signora."

To pay me back for this, she decided to teach me a lesson. She waited until Mr. Hunter was gone, then she dragged me down to the basement and tied my thumbs to a hook above my head. I hung there, half dead from fear and unbearable pain. Then she burned my tongue with a red-hot fork.

So, when Pa's visit with me ended, he was still oblivious to what was going on; and when he got back home, he proudly told everyone what a good upbringing I was getting from my "aunt."

The day after Pa left, Aunt Signora paid the wages owed to the girl she'd hired to take my place, and once again, all of the work fell on my shoulders.

A few years passed in the Hunter household until one day when the couple got into a fight—a knockdown, drag-out affair. They'd had quarrels before, but never this nasty from what I had witnessed. They threw fisticuffs, chairs, plates, and bottles into the action. Aunt Signora cried and cried. As soon as Mr. Hunter left for town on business, she told me to pack her things. By nightfall, we were on the train to Washington proper. There, Aunt Signora arranged for me to work as a nanny for a certain Mrs. Arsinus. I was twelve years old.

I was to look after Mrs. Arsinus's children for two dollars a week, a huge salary to me. After all, it was the first time I would earn anything for my work. I already knew what I wanted to buy with my first pay: shoes. As I took the children out on walks, I eagerly looked into storefront windows and decided on what I fancied.

At the end of my first workweek, Mrs. Arsinus gave me the day off, a Sunday; but she didn't pay me. I was too timid to ask for my salary. I got dressed and shyly shifted from foot to foot, hoping she'd notice me; but she just said, "Why don't you go outside, Maggie? I don't want your aunt to think that I'm making you work on Sunday."

My heart sank; I had to leave with nothing. I didn't even have money for a tram, and I went on foot to my "aunt's" place. She wasn't at home, so I sat there, waiting for her. She walked in wearing makeup, an elegant new dress, and a cheerful smile.

My heart contracted with pain, but I said, "I have no shoes, Aunt Signora. Mrs. Arsinus didn't pay me for this week. Please buy me shoes."

"What's this about shoes? I'll buy you some shoes when time permits. I won't let you waste your money. Mrs. Arsinus will be handing your salary over to me."

I was dumbfounded. I had thought I'd be in charge of my earnings. Instead, not only did I see none of my money, but I didn't get any shoes that week or the next. All of my hopes and dreams scattered like dust. I no longer looked into the store windows making plans; but I understood that I needed to get away from "Auntie."

The thought of leaving came to me all of a sudden, and it seemed to be my only way out. I couldn't picture how to make that happen though. The big, noisy city outside of the confines of Mrs. Arsinus's home scared me, and people seemed alien and unkind.

At this time, Mrs. Arsinus lost her cook and she herself fell ill. Like usual one morning, I dressed the children and informed Mrs. Arsinus that I was taking them out for a walk.

But she lay in bed. She rose up and said sweetly, "Maggie, my child, come here. I want you to cook something for Mr. Arsinus. The cook left us yesterday, and I'm sick."

I readily agreed. I wanted her to know how well I could

cook. Downstairs, in the kitchen, I faced a mess of pots and pans. I made breakfast and put everything in such order that it all shone. Mrs. Arsinus walked into the kitchen, and her jaw dropped in awe.

"This is incredible! I had no idea you were so clever."

From that day on, I was "the cook." The couple hired a new nanny for the children. She was a kind, elderly black woman who could read. At my request, she sometimes looked through the newspaper classifieds to see if someone needed a nanny or a maid. I was aiming to get away from Mrs. Arsinus so that I could free myself from "Auntie."

I found a suitable place. They wanted a Negro girl, aged fourteen, to work as a dishwasher for three dollars a week. I cut out the ad and went to the indicated address in Washington the following Sunday.[16]

I fidgeted as I neared the house. In addition to the fact that I wasn't fourteen yet, they might not like me either. I walked past the house many times before approaching it. For some reason, I liked the look of the place and that made me want the job more. Finally, I summoned some courage and pressed the doorbell. A tall black servant answered and led me to the mistress of the house.

The first question I had to answer was: "How old are you?"

I didn't bat an eye and said, "Fourteen."

"You can't be," the mistress responded dubiously.

Tears sprang to my eyes. The mistress smiled and said, "Well, what's with these tears, girl? I like you." After this brief exchange, she hired me on as a dishwasher for two dollars and fifty cents a week.

That night, I folded my things and slipped away, off to work for my new mistress, Mrs. Davis.

To please Mrs. Davis, I worked hard and tried to delight the cook. I peeled potatoes for her and generally helped in the kitchen. Also, I cleaned up around the bedrooms, although that wasn't part of my duties.

The only person that I didn't like was Watson, the white waiter. Sometimes, if I was alone with him, he'd try to hug me and say things I didn't understand. I didn't go to school like other children did, and I had no friends. I didn't know anything about sexual relations and had never heard anything about love either. I didn't like Watson bothering me, and his face, with its wayward eyes, scared me.

Over the first three weeks working for Mrs. Davis, I didn't get paid in money, but she bought me shoes, underwear, and a dress, and she always gave me money for a tram whenever I wanted to go somewhere on Sundays. I dressed well now; unfortunately, Watson became more of a pain too. I didn't know how to get rid of him.

Finally, I decided to talk about it with our cook, who was also black.

"Mrs. Turner," I asked, "what should you do when someone catches you in the dark, starts kissing and smothering you, and you don't like it?"

My question so overwhelmed this kind, old lady that she dropped a plate. She made me tell her all about Watson's overtures, then she spent the rest of the day sighing and grumbling.

In the evening, she brought the matter up.

"Maggie," she said, "you're facing a heap of trouble. I have to warn you because you are still young and inexperienced and you have no one to take care of you. I'll tell you a story from my past, and let it be a lesson to you.

"I also grew up on my own, like you. Like you, I worked from dawn to dusk, but my workload was even worse. I worked on a farm. I milked the cows, cooked, did laundry, and grazed the cattle in the woods.

"I worked on a huge estate. Pa was a sharecropper and didn't live around us. Even if he had lived nearby, he couldn't have helped me. We were all at the mercy of the master and had nowhere to go.

"The master had two adult sons. The elder often pestered me when I was alone. Late one evening, I was looking for a stray cow in the woods. On the way back, someone grabbed me. He tried to change his voice, but I recognized him immediately. It was the master's son. I tried to fight him off, but he said he had a gun.

"What could I do? He took me by force. I could not go to my father. He had twelve children, not counting me. I told my mother what had happened, but she just cried and told me to go back to the estate. If my father were to take it into his head to intercede on my behalf, he'd have been kicked off the master's land and then hauled into jail on some false charge.

"From then on, the master's son would always wait for me in the dark and he'd take me whenever he wanted. I didn't tell my mother about it anymore. Before long, I found out I was pregnant. I was fourteen years old.

"It didn't take long for the mistress of the house to notice. She cursed me, called me a whore, and kicked me out of the house. I didn't tell her that the child would be from her son. It wouldn't do me any good. I'd still be blamed for everything.

"I heard that there was a free maternity ward in Richmond and decided to go there on foot. But on the way, I felt unwell. An old Negro found me lying in the dust by the road and took me in. His wife looked after me as if I were her own daughter. I gave birth to a son in their care. After I recovered a bit, these lovely people said that they'd be willing to foster the child. I agreed since I had no other option. I never saw my son again. I only know that he lives in Virginia and works on a plantation as a sharecropper.

"So there, Maggie," the cook said in conclusion, "that's what's out in the world. Remember my story, and learn from it. I'll talk to Watson myself."

Whatever she said to Watson, it worked. He quit pestering me. He even began teaching me how to read and write, which made me happy.

Several weeks passed, when suddenly one day, like a bolt from the blue, Aunt Signora swooped in. Scared, I ran into the kitchen. Grasping Mrs. Davis's dress, I pleaded with her: "Please hide me! Don't let her inside!" My teeth chattered, and tears rolled down my face.

They let Aunt Signora in anyway. She walked into the kitchen and said in a sugared tone, "Maggie, darling, where have you been? I've missed you so much!" She reached out to kiss me, but I evaded her and hid behind Mrs. Davis.

Mrs. Davis said, "I don't know what's going on here, but Maggie is scared to death of you. Who are you and why are you here?"

"I'm taking the girl home," Aunt Signora said. "I want her to go to school. Why should she be working? I have my own apartment and plenty of work, and I can take care of her."

I don't know where I got the courage just then. I said, my voice trembling, "No, Aunt Signora. I'm not going with you. Mrs. Davis has bought me clothes and shoes, and I have to pay her back. If Mrs. Davis can't send me to school, I'd rather not even go."

Aunt Signora tried and tried to talk me into leaving, but I remained adamant. Then she started threatening me. "I don't want to, but if I have to I'll take this matter up in court."

But in the end, she didn't go to court. I had yet to learn the extent of her vengefulness.

Seeing that I was determined not to return to her, she came up with another way to get me to leave Mrs. Davis. I was young and naïve, and it wasn't hard for her to trick me.

On one of her visits, in an agitated voice she said that she had received a very sad letter from my father. He'd fallen ill, and he wanted me to come back home right away. This news so upset me that it didn't even occur to me to ask "Auntie" for the letter. I hastily packed and bade Mrs. Davis farewell.

I left Washington that very day.

Chapter 5

Burning Crosses

Whites on the right, Blacks on the left. No mixing![17]

Wasn't it you, gentlemen of the Supreme Court of the United States, who with one stroke of the pen struck out the Bill of Rights as allegedly contrary to the Constitution? What this meant: separate schools for whites and blacks. Seats set aside for "coloreds." Even tenderhearted Christian churches felt the need to divvy up their flock.

It was probably a day like any other when thirteen-year-old Margaret, my future grandmother, stepped off the train at an ordinary station in the South.

It was a rather long walk to my father's cabin from the station, which had been built since I was last here. I knew that my sister Mallisia lived nearby. I visited her first.

Mallisia resided in a small log cabin with a single window, much like Pa's, except that hers had a wooden floor. When I saw her, I didn't recognize the girl she had been. She was fat now and had aged a lot. She had two wonderful children and a kind husband who worked hard to support the family. She knew nothing about Pa, but she filled me in on how our brothers and sisters were doing.

Brother Charles had gone to West Virginia to work in the mines. He couldn't find a job there, and after many struggles, he'd moved to the North. Now, he lived in New York City.

Soon after I'd left, Pa had sent Clara off to live with that relative, but she'd suffered so much there that he'd had to take her back. Now, she worked on a farm a few miles from Mallisia's home.

Brother Patrick had been living with Pa, helping him on the land. The results of their labor weren't enough to feed the both of them, however, so he had opted to work as a farmhand on a neighboring farm.

I stayed with Mallisia for two days, then I visited Clara at a Mrs. Harvey's farm. Clara and I laughed so much and so loudly from our joy in being together, prompting Mrs. Harvey to come downstairs to see what was going on. She had a ten-year-old daughter who didn't want to leave my side when she found out that I lived in Washington. The daughter's pushiness put me off though. Moreover, she demanded that I call her "Miss Andriena" and show her some respect.

When evening fell and Clara had finished her work, we spent a long time relaxing in the yard, reminiscing about our childhood. They were bringing the cows in from the fields, and a farm laborer, William, started milking them. He was very handsome. I liked his thick, curly hair and smooth, dark complexion. I figured either his mom or dad was white.

In the deepening twilight, a woman's form flashed past the farm fence. Seeing her, William began to work so quickly that I couldn't follow the movement of his fingers.

"That's Hattie," Clara said quietly. "She loves William."

"But she's white," I said. Then Clara related to me the sad story of a young black man's love for a white girl.

Hattie's family lived next door next to Mrs. Harvey's farm. Hattie's family was so poor that the younger children had to go around begging for handouts from the other farms. Hattie helped her father in the field and ran the entire household. She was, according to Clara, a very sweet, modest girl, and William had fallen madly in love with her. "They can't live without each other," said Clara. "Every day, they rendezvous."

"Does her ma know about the two of them?"

"Oh yes. Her ma and pa don't have anything against him. They both like him. Her ma even told him that if only they lived somewhere else, then he'd be welcome to visit them — but not here in the South. He can't visit them here. That would only bring a heap of trouble."

As we sat there chatting, William walked up with a bucket of milk.

"Here's some milk for you, Clara," he said with a smile. His teeth were white, and they were smooth like kernels of corn on the cob. He looked so good. I couldn't take my eyes off of him.

The white girl was waiting for him at the fence, and soon he ran over to meet her. Hand in hand, they walked slowly along the road until they disappeared from view.

The next day, I bade my sister farewell and headed for Pa's place. He lived in the same cabin as before, but the porch was new, although the chimney pipe listed even more.

Pa was sitting on the porch chewing tobacco. Upon seeing me, his face brightened. Life had been hard on him; he looked dirty and unkempt, and the cabin was horribly neglected. He didn't appear to be ailing, however, which meant that, of course, Aunt Signora had deceived me.

Just the same, Pa was greatly altered. He looked shorter than he once had. Wrinkles covered his face, and his shoulders sagged; but his hair, gray eyes, and the sad line of his mouth looked the same as before.

He'd cracked a rib while working in the garden. The hoe had caught on a root, and the handle had broken off as he'd tried to tug it free, hitting him in the rib. From then on, he was even more hunched over. To top it off, he was past eighty now.

I decided to remain at home and help him out. Soon, I found a job. Workers were bringing in the harvest at a nearby plantation owned by a Dr. Wells. For fifteen cents a day, they hired me to help. The work started at dawn and went into the evening.

Dr. Wells had a foreman named Miles. He had us all line up in a row and was adamant about no one lagging behind. He reminded me of Pa in that he didn't know the meaning of exhaustion. As I worked, the sharp leaves of the cornstalks cut my hands. By noon, I developed a backache. It hurt so badly that I didn't know if I'd make it to nightfall. Meanwhile, Miles kept up the pace as if he was an automaton, not a man.

When we wrapped up work, total night had descended.

Dr. Wells would ride around his property on horseback. Whenever we crossed paths, he would ask his foreman, "Well, Miles, how'd it go today?" Anyone who didn't manage to keep up with Miles would be fired on the spot.

I couldn't keep pace with him. After working on the plantation for a few days, I didn't feel well at all. That's when Miles said, "Margaret can't keep up, so let's have her bring the water. Ten cents a day."

So, I worked a month at Dr. Wells's plantation. After the corn and tobacco were harvested, we workers were all let go. Then I started working in the household of Mr. Horsely, who ran a farm. I would spend the night at home. Patrick worked as a farm laborer nearby and would come home every night too. We didn't want to leave Pa alone. Soon, Clara left her mistress and joined us. She had become tired of being treated poorly.

Fred, the eldest son of my employer, taught at the Negro school on Sundays. He was a kind young man with a big heart.

It took a great deal of courage to teach black children. Fred possessed just that: courage. Many plantation owners around there demanded that he quit teaching "niggers," but he steadfastly refused to give up his Sunday classes. So, they kicked him out of the school for white children.

Despite this, Fred started an evening school for black children in his pa's barn. The black woodworkers made desks for the children and renovated the space slated for the "school." Mrs. Horsely provided a wood-burning stove, which they installed. They cleaned the space and whitewashed it. Fred procured some textbooks. In the end, forty-eight students attended his school, including men, women, and teenagers. My brother Pat and I were among them.

One day, I mentioned to Pat that I no longer wanted to go to church. He got angry. "Margaret, how can you say such a thing? I'm just glad my other sisters aren't like you. That's what living in the city did to you. Just wait until I tell Pa how godless you are!"

"Pa won't mind. He doesn't even go to church."

Pat had nothing to say to that. You see, as the years passed, Pa had lost his faith, totally and irrevocably.

Fred's school was up and running for a while when someone sent him an anonymous letter warning him that if he didn't stop "messing around with the niggers" he'd find himself in a heap of trouble. "We don't need no nigger lovers around here," the message said. Fred simply acquired a revolver and kept on teaching us.

Then one day, one of the students showed up late to class. He was very worked up and said that as he was climbing the hill to the school, he spied three suspicious-looking people hiding behind the barn.

"Well," said one of the students, "we number forty-eight strong, so I think we can take care of ourselves."

We all armed ourselves with sticks; but Fred said, "Hey, friends, calm down. No one's going to hurt us. Let's get back to work again."

Nobody could concentrate though. Everybody's ear was tuned into the sounds outside. After class ended, we filed outdoors only to see a burning cross right in front of the door. The Ku Klux Klan! Many of the students broke off attending the school from then on.

Classes continued intermittently until one night when the

Klan set fire to the school itself and it burned down with all the textbooks. At that point, Mrs. Horsely was so terrified that she pleaded with her son to simply leave. After digging his heels in for some time, he finally agreed to her request. First, though, he brought all of his students together and told them that he was going to law school.

"After I graduate," he said, "I'll come back here and work as a lawyer. I'll defend poor blacks from the tyranny of plantation owners."

Later on, I found out that he kept his word.

I quit working for Mrs. Horsely, who, after her son left, no longer needed me around. Then, I started working for a Mrs. Wilson, who lived in town. It was a heavy workload. I not only took care of the children, I also did housecleaning and helped out Betty, the cook.

Mrs. Wilson's son was about fifteen and slept in his own room at the far end of the house. His friend, who was a little older, would stay with him.

One morning, I was cleaning their room when their son walked in. I didn't pay any attention to him. Suddenly, the lock clicked, and startled, I turned around. He stood there taking off his jacket and staring at me with a stupid grin. I rushed to the door. A struggle broke out between us, but I managed to get away from him.

I decided to tell his grandmother, a blind woman who sat in the kitchen to "oversee" the work there, about the incident. I should have saved my breath.

"How dare you say such things?" she shrieked. "My grandson wouldn't even look at you, you nasty nigger girl! If you ever say another word about this, I'll have you put in jail. You'd best not say anything to his mother! Get out of here, you little hussy!"

I fled the kitchen without opening my mouth. I sat down on the porch, hands over my ears, and thought things through. I remembered Pa's words! "A poor black man doesn't have to commit a crime to go to jail. All he has to do is displease his white boss man, and he'll be tossed in jail for stealing something. Just let him smile at a white girl he's known since they were children, and he'll be sent to jail for attempted rape." Here this old blind woman was threatening me with jail for telling her about her grandson's misconduct. Yes, Pa was right.

One night, an episode would prompt me to no longer keep quiet about what had happened.[18] I was lying awake with eyes wide open near the cook. Betty and I both slept on the floor in the hallway. Suddenly, a floorboard creaked, then a shadow crept toward us, closer and closer. I screamed. A man took off running, and I recognized him: He was the son's friend. My scream woke Betty up, and she said, "Margaret, I'm so glad you're awake! Every night, he bothers me."

"You haven't told anyone about it?"

"I can't. He has a gun in his pocket. Anyway, the mistress wouldn't believe me. What can I do?"

My scream had awakened everyone in the house. People opened the doors in the hallway, asking, "What's going on? What happened?"

I said, "Someone was creeping up to us."

Betty quickly added, "Margaret must've been having a bad dream. I didn't hear anything."

The next day, Betty and I had a long talk. I told her what the son had attempted to do to me.[19]

She said, "You're still young, Margaret. When you grow up, you'll come to see that you have to work for white masters all your life and that it's futile to struggle. If it's not the mistress's husband, then it'll be her brother, and if not her brother, then the father or some other no-good scoundrel. You'll end up having to submit to him."

"Betty," I said, "when I grow up, I'm going to marry the man I love, regardless whether he is black or white."[20]

"Silly you! No white man will ever marry you. He may

live with you, come to you every night and give you presents. But marry you! That won't happen. I can't tell you what it's all about; but it seems to me that there can never be real love between white and black."

I totally disagreed with Betty. However, she had more life experience, and the evidence was on her side.

Living in the South became ever the more unbearable for me. I felt like in the North, blacks lived more freely.

Mallisia told me that our sister Sarah Jean had married and moved with her husband to Philadelphia. I wrote to Sarah Jean, asking if she'd let me move in with them, and, subsequently, it was decided that I would. But Mrs. Wilson asked me to stay on for two more weeks and promised me an extra two dollars of pay. I needed the money, so I agreed to her offer. For the rest of my life, I have regretted that decision.

Mrs. Wilson sent me off to deliver some things to her sister, on the edge of town. As I sat on the porch waiting for her sister to respond, the sheriff ran by.

When I returned to Mrs. Wilson's, tension punched the air. Everyone was gathering, talking about how a black man had raped a white girl somewhere in the mountains. They said the black man had threatened the girl with a gun. Supposedly, someone even heard her screaming. Vigilantes began looking for the black man. Some men started going from house to house. One of them visited Mrs. Wilson.

I was sitting on the porch with her when one of the irate men showed up. He asked her to send me away so that he could talk to her alone. After leaving the porch, I hovered outside the door, but I couldn't make out their words; but then I heard Mrs. Wilson say, "No, no! You mustn't do it! My brothers won't go!" She burst into tears.

The man left.

Mrs. Wilson's brothers started comforting her. "Sister, you needn't worry so much," I heard one of them say. "We won't go. It's just a boy they're talking about. I thought it was a grown man."

At dinner, nobody had much of an appetite. An oppressive silence reigned. Even the old witch, the grandmother, sat in silence. The thought of the impending violence so preoccupied me that I left my work unfinished. Nobody said anything to me. Meanwhile, Betty silently worked on the dinner.

I asked her, "Betty, who was the sheriff looking for? Do you know?"

She shook her head. "No, I don't. But after we eat, I'll go find out."

I brought in Mrs. Wilson's tea then, prompting her to abruptly stop talking to her brothers, none of whom would look me in the eye. Mrs. Wilson was lying in her bed while both of her brothers sat nearby.

After dinner, Betty departed. I felt completely depressed. The house seemed so dark and gloomy. The wind howled through the trees like a roaring crowd.

Soon, Betty came back. She told me that the "cad" was still on the loose.

"He lives on the other side of the mountain," Betty said. "Several men came from that direction. They were going from house to house talking to everybody."

"They're lying. It can't be true. They must be lying. First, they said he had a gun, but now it turns out he's known the girl since they were children."

At that, a terrible foreboding came over me. I recalled the young man with the soft voice that I met beyond the mountain. It couldn't be! I did my best to banish the feeling of doom. I put the children to bed, but I couldn't get to sleep myself. Betty and I sat in the kitchen, and I told her about the young man who lived on the far side of the mountain—the young man who was in love with a white girl.

Some time passed. We could hear a mob outside the nearby courthouse. I lay my head on the table and fell asleep. Suddenly, someone was shaking me awake. "Margaret, Margaret!" Betty said as she roused me.

A crowd had gathered in front of the house. We filed down the dark hallway to French doors that opened out onto the veranda with a view of the moon-illuminated yard. A young black man sat in back of the sheriff's ride. I couldn't make out their faces. From the veranda, we heard the young man begging for mercy.

"I didn't hurt anyone. Why do you want to kill me? I'm still young. I don't want to die. Give me a trial. Hattie will tell you. I didn't do anything to her. My poor mama!"

His voice was so soft and pleading. I recognized it right away. It *was* William! The mob was about to rip him apart!

I heard his last words: "Put me in jail. Why are you handling me over to that mob? Poor, poor Hattie!"

Someone conked him on the head with the butt of a gun, and I heard a "crack." "Unnh!" William groaned and fell silent. My eyes grew dim. I screamed in despair and sank to the floor. Betty rushed up and dragged me into the house.

From that time on, I hated the South and the Southerners. On that day, the people of Lovingston, Virginia, slaughtered an innocent young man who was not yet eighteen years old. Out of the crowd of over two hundred people, not a single person raised a voice in his defense. Nobody said, "No! Don't kill him!" They all howled like wild beasts demanding his blood. The sheriff handed the sacrificial victim over to the crowd like he was throwing a piece of meat to a pack of ravenous dogs. Three white men up to no good had falsely accused him of raping Hattie, a white girl. Later, I talked to Hattie myself and heard all the details about the bloodlust.

A local plantation owner, Thacker, had been after Hattie for a long time, threatening to go after William if she didn't submit to him. On the eve of that evil day, Hattie went to town to pick up a few things at the store. The road led past the plantation where William worked. He and Hattie chatted a bit over the fence. After William heard about how Thacker was harassing Hattie, he decided to escort her. Dusk was falling as they passed through the woods. Suddenly, three men leaped out from behind some bushes and grabbed William. Although it was already dark, Hattie could tell that one of them was Thacker. William shouted, "Run, Hattie, run!" He managed to break free and get away himself, but nobody pursued him. They wanted Hattie.

The next day, all around town people were saying that three white men had caught William trying to rape a white girl.

Hattie was crying as she told me this.

... nor shall any State deprive any person of life, liberty, or property, without due process of law.

I, James Lloydovich Patterson, grandson of Margaret, cite the Fourteenth Amendment to the Constitution of a country where pogroms and lynchings are commonly carried out with the help of local authorities and the police.

Ku Klux Klan!

The word sounds like a curse!

Ku Klux Klan!

They're covered by white robes that signify their lawlessness, their twisted souls, and their craven cowardice.

"We took it upon ourselves to fight for the ideals originally put forth by Adolf Hitler ..."

"We openly declare that we're aiming to throw hundreds of thousands of Jews into the gas chambers ..."

"We recognize the superiority of the white man over the Negro. We are proud of this superiority and will never allow these lower human beings to usurp the rights won for us by the blood and genius of our white ancestors ..."

"We will do whatever is necessary to ensure the purity of the races."

Now, I use my imagination to infiltrate the gatherings of modern vigilantes in Texas, Georgia, Arkansas, and South Carolina. I can discern in a raging mob the governor of one of these states, repeating like a prayer the oaths of the secret order. I see the judge cloaked by the darkness of night exchanging his black judicial robes for a pointed hood, with a thin slit for his eyes.

An ominous cross looms over them, and in those flames, all that is good and all that embodies hope are engulfed, as each minute generates alienation and anger, marking the rebirth of fascism.

Chapter 6

Why the Liberty Bell Is Mute

One of Philadelphia's chief tourist attractions is the Liberty Bell. This historic relic, say the history books, first rang during the public reading of the Declaration of Independence.

I can't imagine the full extent of racial savagery when, in this day and age, under the law of the state of Texas, a colored girl does not have the right to play a "romantic role" opposite a white boy, and when, in the city of Monroe, North Carolina, two preteen Negro boys are put on trial for "attempted violence against a woman" simply because a white girl kissed one of them while playing. When, in Louisiana, a new law is enacted prohibiting the transfusion of black blood to white people and vice versa for fear of alleged "infection from black blood." But even before my grandmother was born, hasn't segregation in the United States always been clearly one-sided?

Sarah Jean hadn't lived with us since she was a child. I hardly knew her. She was the closest person to me in Philadelphia.

In just a few days after moving in with her, I found a job working for a doctor for five dollars a month; but then the doctor's nephew tried to molest me. When I raised a complaint to the doctor, he accused me of seducing his nephew. That very day, I got my things together and left.

A month passed, then another. I went through several jobs. Sometimes, I'd earn eight dollars a month. Other times, I had to make do with three.

While on a trip with one of my employers outside Philadelphia, I received a letter from Pat. He wrote to say that Pa had died. Pat also related that he was abandoning Pa's plot of land and going to New York to move in with our brother Charles.[21]

I sobbed like a little girl over Pat's letter. My poor father! I couldn't even make it back to have one final look at him. Despair tore my heart asunder.

I felt completely alone. No one else really loved me like Pa had. I needed love and affection so much right then!

These were dark days. A woman who'd hired me to travel with her outside of Philadelphia abandoned me in some little town and stiffed me on a month's salary. Only with great effort did I manage to return to the city, where I moved back in with Sarah Jean and started to look for another job. But I ran out of luck. I visited different agencies for two months straight and couldn't find a thing. Nobody wanted to hire me. So, I started doing laundry at home for the main hospital. I washed sheets and linen from sunrise to sunset. In just a few weeks, the skin started peeling off my hands.

Then, a stroke of good fortune fell my way. At the employment office, I caught the eye of a young, richly attired lady who was looking for a maid. For some reason, out of the wealth of young black women searching for work that day, this woman, a Mrs. Peters, settled on me.

Mrs. Peters's husband was in the insane asylum. The couple didn't have any children.

Part of my job was to accompany her on trips. She didn't linger long anywhere. We stayed the longest in Boston, and that was for two or three weeks. Mrs. Peters would rent a few rooms in a hotel. This is what other wealthy people did as well. So there would be a lot of maids in these places, and they all got to know each other. One of them, a woman named Flora, invited me to go with her to a party.

"Maggie," she said, "wear your best dress."

I showed her my dresses, and she said, "No, none of these dresses will do. You have to buy yourself a nice dress."

With her help, I bought my first evening gown. I looked nice in it, and Flora thought I'd make a good impression on everyone at the party.

At first, Mrs. Peters didn't want to let me go. Finally, she said, "Well, okay. Only be careful, Maggie. Don't let yourself get drunk. After all, isn't this your first real party?"

"Yes, Mrs. Peters."

When I got to Flora's room, I discovered two other girls who were also going to the party. Their appearance stunned me. Their faces were painted and powdered, and they wore dresses with slits up to the knees. Their loud appearance put me off.

Flora wanted to paint my face, but I adamantly refused. Then one of the painted ladies said, "Hey, she's still so young, she doesn't need any makeup. Let's just fix her hair."

A car came for us. We traveled a long way along bustling, brightly lit streets. Finally, the car pulled up at a luxurious mansion to the sounds of a band spilling out of the windows.

As we walked up the stairs, I didn't see any men; but as soon as we entered the hall, I gasped. White men, all wearing elegant suits, filled the room. They were dancing and flirting with black girls, and laughter filled the air. I stood stock-still, confused and shocked. Flora noticed. She whispered to me, "This is where you can experience true pleasure such as you've never known before. All of these men are very wealthy. All you have to do is catch the eye of one of them, and you'll never have to work again."

I turned around to leave then, but Flora grabbed my arm.

"Margaret, don't be a fool. Hundreds of girls, black and white, do it. This might be your lucky day. If you leave, you'll wreck the entire party for us. You see, there's one girl for each man here."

I summoned my courage and said, "Why didn't you tell me what kind of party this is? I don't want to be some rich man's plaything. I already work for them and have my entire life. Look, they're all white. None of these men would marry me."

Flora looked at me in surprise and said, "Marry you? Most of them are already married."

"So, what they want then is a black girl to love for just a night? I won't go for it."

Someone called Flora over, and she ran to him. She, apparently, was having a fine time. She chatted, laughed, and appeared to be happy. I heard one of the other girls say to her, "You should know better than to bring along such a little fool. Now you've done it."

The bright lights and intoxicating scent of flowers made me dizzy. My head was whirling. Couldn't I just dance with these men? Talk to them? Feel at ease with them? I thought about Pa's disfigured hand. Before my mind's eye drifted the pale shadow of a young man ripped apart by a mob. I turned and walked down the stairs. A heavy curtain covered the entrance to a small room that looked like the restroom in a theater. I walked in and sat in the corner.

Girls ran up and down the stairs, laughing merrily. One of them looked at me. As she fixed her hair before the mirror, she said, "Honey, come with me. Let's have some fun. As you went up the stairs, a very rich man down there spotted you and wanted to meet you. He hasn't selected a girl yet. He wants you. Don't be silly. Let's go down there."

I said, "I would like to go home."

The next morning, when I helped Mrs. Peters get dressed, the first thing she said was, "Well, Maggie, how was your party?"

Blushing and averting my eyes, I told her everything. After a long pause, she said, "You're a good girl, Maggie, and I want to save you from making a big mistake. I see in your face a hatred of all whites without exception. That's not fair. Many whites are against the lynch mob, but we can't do anything about it because in America, the power lies in the hands of the rich. They pit the poor, white and black, against each other. This makes it easier for them to control things."

My face clearly expressed my astonishment, and Mrs. Peters understood how my thoughts were overwhelming me.

"You're surprised by what I'm saying, Maggie," she said. "What you don't know is that when I was very young, I was poor, just like you. I worked in a dry goods store as a clerk. All of my money now comes from my husband. He bought me when I was seventeen years old. It happened at my first party. He got me so drunk that I was past the point of sentience. He kept me in his room for days. But I didn't make it easy for him to get away from me after that. He had to marry me. So you see, Maggie, white girls are bought and sold just like black girls."

I couldn't believe my ears, but she was telling me the truth. I thought about Mrs. Baldwin, who so kindly took the place of our mother. Then there was Fred, our teacher. He too was a true friend to poor blacks.

A year passed. I felt a strong desire to see my family, so one day I bade Mrs. Peters farewell and boarded a train bound for New York.

As I passed through Philadelphia, where my grandmother once stayed, the silhouette of the decrepit Liberty Bell with its corroded copper tongue flickered fast. Later, somewhere in Missouri, a heavy blow knocked me off my feet. I was left lying on the street as heavy steps beat a retreat. The rhythmic footsteps echo in my consciousness like the ringing of a bell. The Liberty Bell.

Chapter 7

In New York

Suffer, suffer
Die on earth,
Starve, you'll get to heavenly paradise.
There you'll get a loaf and tea!
—Joe Hill[22]

I'm going down to the Bowery. In the early days, the rumble of
overpasses didn't exist, nor the humdrum of the myriad sounds of
life and the reflections of the neon advertisements. It was the haven
of American knaves, the inhabitants of the depths of New York
City. I felt troubled by thoughts of how, half a century ago, Grand-
ma Margaret's brothers, Charles and Patrick, wasted away while
seeking odd jobs ...

The sight of my brother Charles took me aback. He was a
good-looking young man when last I'd seen him years earlier. Now, I didn't even recognize him. One side of his face
was skeletal, his mouth on that side in a perpetual frown.
The other side looked like that of the old Charlie I knew. He
also had a large lump on his head that he covered by growing his hair long. He'd been in a work accident during the
construction of the subway, and part of his cheekbone had
been surgically removed.

He had an apartment on Third Avenue on the east side
of town. It was, in fact, a dirty, narrow hallway lined with
hovels that they called suites. A small barbershop stood next

to his room—this was Charlie's business. He'd established himself as a barber.

Clara also lived in New York, in an apartment in Harlem. She'd married a young black man from back home.

Charlie suggested that I quit my job and move in with him, and I did. Soon, Pat moved in with us too. I lived in this wretched house with my brothers for three years. I did the housework and was very happy. Charlie taught me how to cut hair, and I often helped him in his shop.

Pat worked on a nearby construction site driving the mules. I'd bring him his lunch at noon.

One day, I showed up with his food, but I couldn't find him. I asked everybody about his whereabouts, but nobody could tell me. That day, he didn't come home either. All night long, I waited for him by the open window.

The next day, I again unsuccessfully sought him out. Tired and frustrated, I returned to the barbershop.

Just then, one of our regular clients walked in. "Well, how is your brother?" he asked. "Was he badly hurt?"

That's how we found out that Pat had been injured. He had fallen into a pit. The mule he'd been driving didn't survive, but by some miracle Pat had, although he'd broken many bones. He spent three months in the hospital and couldn't work for an entire year after that. The company building the subway he'd been working for gave him a three hundred dollar payout, which wasn't even enough to cover his medical bills. So, Charlie and I had to feed him. To earn much-needed income, I began to take in seamstress work. This provided us a few more dollars a month.

We lived near a Negro church with a Sunday school. I really liked the lessons at this school. We often put on plays and organized excursions to museums and walks in the country. Among the students were lots of other young people whose company I enjoyed. Sometimes, we threw parties full of dancing and singing.

At one of these parties, I met a young man named Archie Patterson. Archie struck me as very nice. He was outgoing, cheerful, and smart. Everybody liked him. A couple of days after we met, he dropped by my apartment. I was happy to see him, and we chatted awhile. We'd go out in the evenings on walks.

Frequently, Charlie would say, "Margaret, I don't like Mr. Patterson coming by here to see you so often." When I told Archie what my brother had said, he proposed to me immediately. I was at a loss and asked Archie to talk to Charlie. Just as I expected, Charlie told me, "You still don't know each other well. Wait until autumn. If you find your feelings have deepened, I'll agree to the marriage."

But Archie kept pleading with me not to wait until fall. I loved my brother and didn't want to upset him, but my love for Archie continued to blossom. So, one day, Archie and I secretly married.[23]

When Charlie found out about our marriage, it deeply saddened him, but he did not reproach me.

At the same time, Archie was making forty-five dollars a month.[24] That allowed us to rent an apartment and save some money. Then business dropped off, and Archie lost his job. We quickly used up our modest savings and had to leave our apartment and move in with Charlie.

After much struggling, I managed to find work as a janitor that came along with a free apartment. Also, I earned extra money by cleaning around the building. Every day, Archie looked for employment. He'd get a one- or two-day job but nothing permanent.

The hard life and struggles to find work left their mark on him. He stopped laughing and singing. He'd come home and wearily sit down with his head in his hands. He could stay like that for hours.

Sometimes, Charlie would come by and say, "Margaret, Archie isn't well. Can't you see? He's lost weight."

But Archie would say, "No, I'm not sick. I'm just very tired."

I talked him into seeing a doctor whose laundry I often took in. After examining him, the doctor said, "Your husband has consumption. If you want him to live, get him out of New York."

I washed clothes for a man named Mr. McKenzie, who had a country house in the Catskills. He was kind enough to offer this place to Archie and me. At the time, Mrs. McKenzie was living there. So, when we arrived, she refused to let Archie in. She feared he'd infect the children.

To our good fortune, we met Mr. Halicus, the only black resident around there. He rented a room out to us, and Archie spent whole days outdoors. Immediately, he started feeling better. Mr. Halicus was a forestry contractor, and Archie cooked for his loggers. I did the laundry for many families in the Catskills, but I barely earned enough to pay for food.

I decided to open up a laundry for the summer months. We needed a horse and wagon to make this happen. It wasn't easy, but Archie and I managed to buy them by agreeing to pay in installments. Archie was feeling so much better and could even help me out.

All summer, I washed laundry from early in the morning until late at night. In autumn, after the summer residents left, my workload plunged. So, we looked after a house for the winter, and in exchange we received a free apartment. Archie landed a job as a driver for the local doctor, and I did all the work for the household: chopping wood, hauling water—things Archie couldn't do anymore.

Times were hard. I was in my twenties and had to support myself and my husband; but Archie was feeling better every day, and it looked like our fortunes might change.

Finally, the day came when we could return to New York.

We rented a cheap apartment on Fifty-sixth Street, on the East Side. They called our building the "house of all nations." Thieves, drunkards, cocaine addicts, and prostitutes lived there. You could hear brawling at all hours of the day or night. Police raids were frequent as were ambulances arriving to take away those injured in the fighting.

Archie was skilled at painting and plastering. He put up posters advertising his services and soon received orders. It wasn't a lot of work, but we managed to get by somehow.

One night, I awoke to hear a terrible scream. I hurried out of bed, opened the door, and found myself engulfed in clouds of hot smoke that burst into the room. The entire building was on fire. Archie and I jumped into our clothes and rushed out onto the landing. Firemen were pounding on the windows, shouting, "Get out of there!" We fought our way down the fire escape.

Now, we had neither an apartment nor property, so we moved in temporarily with Archie's brother, Hugh Patterson. Hugh had three children. Sarah, his wife, worked during the day. I looked after the children while she was gone. Hugh and Sarah provided us with food while Archie sought work, although there too we struggled to make ends meet.

Archie's brother and sister-in-law helped Archie get new tools to replace what he'd lost in the fire. He started getting orders for his services again, so we were able to rent a room in the Bronx.

But Archie started feeling unwell again, and by this time I was pregnant. Work was hard on Archie, but he did all he could to stay on the job for the sake of our future child. Once, he said to me, "Margaret, when is the child due? I'm afraid I'll die before I see the child."

To make matters worse, Pat didn't have any work or money and he moved in with us. Quickly, Archie taught him plastering and they worked together.

Finally, in August 1910, our son was born. Archie took him in his arms and said in a trembling voice, "Son, I hope fortune will smile on you more than it has on your father."

Not long after this, illness hit Archie hard. He was no longer able to work, despite numerous requests for his services. He wanted to go back home to North Carolina to visit his mother, whom he hadn't seen in nineteen years.

So, cradling our baby in our arms and with a few dollars in our pockets, we set off. Archie's mother lived in dire poverty. She was very happy to see us and spent entire days with her grandson. We lived on what I made by doing laundry and other odd jobs.

A month and a half after our arrival, Archie died. His death devastated me, but I had to keep going.[25]

I went back to New York with our four-month-old son, Lloyd. Archie's mother had urged me to leave the child with her, but I didn't want to do that. Lloyd was everything to me now. If I were to have let him go, I'd have been like a ship without a rudder. I knew I had a difficult path before me, but I had purpose in life—to raise my son and make a worthy man out of him.

I returned from the South and moved in with my brother-in-law Hugh. Charlie didn't invite me to stay with him. Ultimately, he couldn't get past how I'd married Archie behind his back, and I was too proud to ask him for help.

So, I embarked on a lengthy search for work. Nobody wanted to hire me because of the baby. Finally, I found something with a society lady. The work was massive—she threw parties and receptions every day. I'd keep Lloyd in the kitchen. I wrapped him up in a blanket on the floor, and I had no time at all to look after him. He caught a cold, fell ill, and nearly died.

After a few months, the lady fired me after I unwittingly betrayed her love affairs to her husband. Then I went back to the Pattersons. But they, too, had no means, so I couldn't remain there.

I was offered work for a certain Mr. Baron, who lived on an estate some thirty miles from New York. It was my only option, so I accepted the position.

That very day, I stepped off the train at a small station. Mr. Baron had sent someone to pick me up. Late that night, we arrived at the estate. The servant took me in to see the master of the house.

From our conversation, I didn't understand how much he'd be paying me. All he said was, "Come see me when you need money."

Many laborers worked on Mr. Baron's farm. I had to have breakfast ready for them by six a.m., so I was up by four. I'd leave my son in bed and couldn't even check on him until eight a.m. By the time he woke up, I was already fixing lunch. So, I saw my child even less than when I worked in the city.

Mr. Baron's farmworkers also didn't get regular wages and constantly fought him over this. Every week, two or three would quit without ever getting paid. Some would try to take him to court, but generally, nothing would come of it. It was too expensive to file a claim, and, anyway, the authorities would side with the employer.

After I settled in at the country estate, I wrote to Charlie. Yes, he was still upset with me, but I loved him just as I did before. He never responded to my letter. But after a while, I received a letter from a friend who would drop in sometimes. She wrote that Charlie was very sick and was in such a bad state of affairs that he couldn't even pay to see a doctor.

I wanted to help him, but I didn't have any money either. So, I decided to talk to the master of the house.

"Mr. Baron," I said, "I need you to pay regular wages, please. I need to send some money to my sick brother."

"You should be glad you have a permanent job," Mr. Baron told me. "Who's going to take you on with a child?"

"Then pay me for what I'm due for the time I've already put in, and I'll be on my way."

But he didn't want me to leave because who would do the cooking then for the workers? He gave me five dollars and said he would pay ten dollars a month. I sent the five dollars to Charlie.

A week later, I heard that Charlie was getting worse, and I decided I just had to see him no matter what. After a huge fight with the master of the house, he gave me another ten dollars. I gathered up my son and walked on foot to the station.

Charlie was so happy when I appeared. He was very ill. In addition to his already-disfigured face, an ulcer had grown on the left side of it. The doctors said he had cancer. I knew my brother didn't have long to live, so I decided not to go back to Mr. Baron's farm. Instead, I settled in with Charlie to care for him.

I took his place as a barber, and it worked out. I was glad that I could help Charlie. After all, he'd helped me when I needed it.

Day by day, his ulcer grew. When Lloyd was one and a half years old, I lost my beloved brother.

I stayed on in his apartment, working in the barbershop, but after paying the rent, I'd have nothing left to live on. So, I started working at a factory.

I was responsible for all of the dirtiest work. I had to mop the floors and clean everything at the end of the workday. For hours, I was on my hands and knees. Quickly, I developed blisters.

The factory workers decided to go on strike. They weren't in a union. Before the strike, they asked me if I would agree to demands for a raise. Of course I agreed, although I had no idea what a strike was.

We chose one worker to negotiate with the others and went with her to see the manager.

"We want to start negotiations," this delegate said. "We can't live on the wages you're paying us. We want a raise to one dollar a week."

The manager looked askance at me and asked, "And what does the Negro girl want?"

"She's with us."

"Then I'll find another cleaning lady today."

I turned to leave, but the workers immediately stood up for me.

"She's one of us!" their voices rang out. "You can't fire her."

The manager smiled and said, "I'll respond to your demands tomorrow morning."

We all went back to our places feeling like the negotiations had gone well. But when we got to work the next day, we found fifty new girls at the factory and one man. He was there to replace me.

The manager said, "Anyone not willing to accept my terms here can see me for their final pay, and I've decided to let some of you go."

He named the leaders of the strike and told me to "get the hell out." Everyone else could stay, but their wages would be reduced by one dollar a week.

The strikers' delegates tried to talk with the new workers and convince them to refuse the work; but virtually all of them had been out of a job for a long time and were in desperate need of money. Still, the striking workers lingered on until the manager called the police, and the police booted us out.

This was my first strike, but my fighting spirit was not yet awakened. All that had happened was that I'd lost my job. Meanwhile, many of the women workers stayed on at the factory despite having to work for even less pay.

Again out of work, I returned to cutting hair. My new employer wouldn't let me bring my child in, so I'd leave

Lloyd with a neighbor. The neighbor, however, often forgot about him. Once, a customer dropped by the barbershop and said, "Is that your son sleeping out there on the street?"

"No," I said. "I leave my son at home. I have a woman taking care of him."

"Someone's kid is out there sleeping in the doorway of a bar. It looks like your son."

I ran outside to look. Yes, it was in fact Lloyd. He was not yet four years old. He knew he wasn't allowed to bother me at work, so he'd come as close as he could and had fallen asleep in the doorway of a nearby bar. My heart broke. I picked up my son, carried him to the barbershop, and told the owner, "If you want me to work for you, you have to let me bring Lloyd along."

From then on, I brought Lloyd with me and put him to sleep in the back room.

One day, two men from Poughkeepsie dropped by the barbershop. One of them asked me, "Are you Mrs. Patterson?"

"Yes."

"Word has it that you're very good with hair. I need a good hairdresser, so I've come to see you. What do you think about moving to Poughkeepsie? I'll pay you a good wage."

I didn't know what to say. Then the man added, "My name is Dixon. I have a barbershop. And this is Mr. Glascoe, my driver."

Just then, Lloyd ran in. "This is my son," I said.

Mr. Dixon patted the boy on the head and said, "It would please me if you agreed to move to Poughkeepsie. I know you'd like it there. I run a very nice barbershop, and my wife could watch your son while you're at work. You could live with us."

I wanted to leave New York, but I was leery about trusting someone I didn't know. My current employer also didn't think I should quit working for him; but after meeting Mr.

Dixon, he bombarded me with letters and telegrams and promised me such impressive benefits that I couldn't resist. So, Lloyd and I moved to Poughkeepsie.

Chapter 8

War

Now that thousands of sons of our people are in military camps and fighting in France, you Negroes may well hope that, as soon as the war is over, you will be granted full civil rights—all the rights that other American citizens enjoy.
—President Woodrow Wilson

Poughkeepsie was a small, cozy town. I liked it. Its people were prejudiced against blacks, but I didn't feel it much. I tried to avoid any conflicts. I was too tired of constantly struggling. Everyone I knew was good to me and to Lloyd, especially Mr. Glascoe, Dixon's driver. He was so good to us that I grew closer and closer to this wonderful man.

On December 24, 1917, I married Steve Glascoe. Five days later, he was taken into the military, along with hordes of others who, like him, were seduced by the fanfare, the waving flags, and banners. He was dispatched to Europe for the slaughter. The day he was to ship off, I left work, and along with everyone else, I went to the station.

Neither my husband, nor I, nor anyone else there had any idea what this war was about and to whose benefit it was either. These were dark, harsh days, and the only thing that I wanted were letters from my husband. When I finally got one, it contained only a few words: "Please write to me. Everyone is getting letters except me." But I'd been writing to him every day. Why wasn't he getting my letters? Every day,

I scanned the newspapers to see if he was listed among the dead or wounded. This went on for nine months. By the end of that time, my hair had turned gray.[26]

Then my husband wrote to me:

My Dearest Wife,

I hope you and our little son are well. I think about you all the time. I'm worried that you're facing difficulties at work since all of the men have gone off to France. Please, let me know when you write back if the government is helping out in any way. I worry about you all the time.

I'm healthy right now, but I am sick and tired of eating beans. I enlisted in the 92nd division, in the sapper detachment, but I'm still a mule driver. You probably read about the general's order in the newspapers. They don't want black soldiers to appear in public. All of us ardently protested over this. I don't know what will come of it.

Back in the States they told us that we'd have black officers, but they're all white. The black officers we signed on with were all transferred to different regiments after we got here. What we're left doing is building barracks, clearing the ground and setting up camp for the troops. Some bigwig in the government said to us, "This is a white man's war." I so wish I could come home, far away from this filthy horror.

The officers try to fire us up with the "fighting spirit." But they're not very successful at this. I don't want to kill anyone; I don't want anyone to kill me.

I read this letter over and over.

American women's clubs and associations tried to keep black women from working for the Red Cross. We knitted stockings, gloves, and sweaters; but to send these things to our loved ones in France, we had to go through the Red Cross. Of course, very often, these items didn't make it to the men.

Once, when a black woman showed up at the workspace

run by the Red Cross, they suggested that she work from home since there wasn't much room there. That prompted us to create our own organization. We called it the Black Cross. We wanted to do our part for the country and not be put down for it.

I had a lot of free time because business was not great at the barbershop. Lloyd was now seven years old and in school.[27] My own childhood had been so difficult and bleak that I wanted things to be better for him. At least he could go to school. When he grew up, he could decide on a profession for himself. Neither I nor my husband had been able to go to school. We were both painfully aware of what a hard lot the uneducated face in the world.

Steve wrote back:

My Dear Wife and Son!

Your letter arrived this morning. I was very lucky it came in the morning, because by noon we were transferred elsewhere. Colonel Haywood started shouting that we were all a bunch of laborers and porters, not soldiers. So they took away our shovels for digging trenches and sent us to the front.

I'm not very happy about this—it means I'm even farther away from you. Some of the American soldiers go out of their way to turn the French against us. The American Young People's Christian Association is especially trying to hurt us.

I got your package—thank you. But I've been assigned to the convoy that carries ammunition, so I'm not allowed to smoke.

Trucks pass us by from the front filled with corpses one after the other. I'm very glad that I'm not called upon to do any killing. But I am part of this war, and it's almost the same thing.

What is it giving me or any of the other poor men who

*are caught up in it? Disease and death—that's about it. But
I understand full well why the rich are all in for this war.
They don't do the fighting, but they reap huge profits from
it. The front is hundreds, even thousands of miles away, and
I'll wager that they are not eating beans every day.*

*But enough about that! If I keep on writing about things
like that, they'll stop giving you my letters ...*

I almost physically felt the endless stream of letters coming from the front from men ripped from their homes, overwhelmed, spun around in the violent whirlpool of war.

In those days when death was everywhere, the nine-
teen-year-old Ernest Hemingway sent a letter from a hastily
equipped field hospital to his family.

*You know, they say that there is nothing fun in this war.
That's the truth. I don't want to say that this is hell, because
these words have been circulating since General Sherman
uttered them ...*

Finally, the war ended. The soldiers were coming home.
Violent demonstrations erupted everywhere. Everyone was
happy that the horror was over, and I was glad too, but not
because the allies had defeated the Germans. I was glad that
my husband was returning home.

Suddenly, his letters broke off again. Whenever a steamer
with black soldiers would arrive from Europe, I'd rush out
from work and hurry to the port to be there when they disembarked. But Steve was never among them.

One evening, I received a telegram stating: "Corporal Ste-
ven Glascoe is gravely ill. He's in the Ellis Island Hospital No.
1."

I went to South Wharf at about seven in the morning. A
small barge carrying workers was leaving for the island. I
asked the captain to let me onto the barge. I told him that I
was in a hurry to see a sick soldier.

"I can't let you on board. This barge is for workers en route to their jobs. Wait here for the ten o'clock ferry."

"My husband might be dead by then!" I cried, pushing past him and jumping onto the barge.

The captain tried to drag me off, but I wouldn't let him. So, willy-nilly, he had to take me to Ellis Island.

When the authorities tell you that a soldier is sick, that means he's near death. After a lengthy search for Steve, I found his ward. He was lying in a long hall lined with bunks on both sides.

Those near death were situated in a far corner of the room. They were transferred there, away from the others, when the doctors abandoned all hope for them. This hell is where I found my Steve! He was so far gone that he could no longer speak. His pallor spoke of deathly illness. Then he saw me, and my arrival snatched him out of death's embrace. The doctor said that had I shown up even an hour later, Steve would likely have perished by then.

When he heard my voice, he roused himself and tried to speak. He looked so happy at hearing me that I couldn't stop crying; but I pulled myself together and spoke to him in a calm voice. Under the rules, I wasn't allowed to stay too long; but every day, I would go to see Steve, and he looked better and better.

After three months of hospitalization, finally I could bring him home. Thanks to my efforts, he'd recovered; but he wasn't the same Steve. Deprivation and illness had impacted his health. He could no longer work as a driver. The doctors told me he wouldn't last long unless I got him out of the city.

We decided to purchase a house in the country closer to nature, so I began saving money. We ate as cheaply as possible and wore our clothes until they were rags. When I got back from the laundry where I worked, I'd wash clothes at the utility sink until late into the night. Steve procured orders for me and would deliver the laundry to each home afterward.

After we saved enough to make a down payment, we found a small house in Westfield, New Jersey, with a white fence around it and flowers everywhere. At first, the realtor wanted nothing to do with "niggers," but then his anger changed to mercy. We had to pay him fifty dollars for this change of heart. After signing the paperwork, we moved to Westfield right away. Two huge cherry trees in bloom rose in the garden outside our house, surrounding us with their scent.

The very first day in our new home, Steve set about preparing the land for a garden. Happily, he worked on that plot every free minute. Our domestic bliss, however, was short-lived. A month after our move, toward the end of June, Steve felt worse. We visited a doctor, who came back with this pronouncement: "We need to operate as soon as possible. Bring him to the hospital tomorrow."

"But then I'll never regain my health," Steve said sadly.

"Never mind. Don't worry. Everything will be fine," the doctor said.

The doctor, however, didn't realize that Steve had been gassed during the war and shouldn't be subjected to ether. Steve died during surgery.

Again, I found myself being a mother and father to Lloyd. He was fifteen years old now, an age where a father is especially needed.[28] He continued with his education. In high school, he struggled in science classes and flunked a grade. He wanted to drop out then and start working somewhere, but I wasn't going to allow him to do that. If he were to quit school, he'd be dooming himself. He'd end up moving from one job to another, just like I did, and live the life of a black person.

I had to find a solution.

What followed were years of study at a black college in Hampton, Virginia, and the times that instilled within my father's soul a spirit of rebelliousness toward anything that degraded human life. The times shaped his character and life path.

Chapter 9

Red and Black

She liked talking to people, she liked listening to their stories about life, and their complaints and doubts. Her heart was overflowing with joy every time she noticed acute discontent in a person, the discontent that protesting against the blows of fate, intensely seeks answers to questions that have already taken shape in the mind.
—Maxim Gorky

I started working for a family as a maid. I lived as frugally as I could and managed to send some of my earnings to Lloyd, who was attending Hampton Institute, in Virginia.[29] In these times, only letters from my son brightened my days.

Lloyd was quite satisfied with the education he was receiving. He was making great strides, and his professors predicted a brilliant future for him. He decided to go into scenic design.

He wrote to me often, sharing details about his life at college and his projects. But not long before he was slated to graduate, he wrote to me, saying,

Dear Mom,
You've probably heard about the strike at the college. We're protesting against the administration's recent refusal to hire Black teachers.
You know, Mom, even though this is a Black college,

there aren't many Black teachers. Of course, the students are all Black, but most of the faculty is White. And we see how the White teachers don't want to sit with the Black students.

You should have seen the outrage that followed when the news spread about one of the White teachers who attended a Ku Klux Klan rally in Norfolk last year. The entire student body demanded that she be fired.

We've selected a committee to organize the strike, and a delegation. The dean refused to see the delegation, so we went on strike. All of us walked out of class. It's so strange now, with all of the classrooms emptied of students and the faculty left with nothing to do!

But the student body is showing extraordinary discipline. We're all in sync, no disorder. We spend half of the day at the stadium. We play football, baseball and other games, and then in the evenings we attend meetings.

Yesterday the dean attended the meeting and delivered a big speech. He went on and on about the college's traditions, and expressed "deep regret" that "the entire student body had fallen under the influence of a small group of rabble-rousers." And then he announced that due to the sad state of affairs, the college would be closed for an indefinite period of time.

We all cheered, hearing this. I'm leaving tomorrow. Meet me at the station.

Once he got back to Westfield, Lloyd started looking for work. Though he was now adept in scenic design, he couldn't find employment. I was out of work then too and had to settle for odd jobs. America was in the midst of an economic crisis: the Great Depression.[30]

Lloyd's unemployment lasted all winter. We lived from hand to mouth. Little by little, Lloyd fell into a state of deep despair. His life seemed to be at a dead end.

By chance, we read in a Negro newspaper that Soviet Russia needed a group of young black people for a film. Lloyd said, "I want to go. I heard that all you have to do is pay your way over there, and then, in Soviet Russia, you can get work right away. Mom, let me go."

I didn't waver for long. The thought of him leaving distressed me, but his despair upset me more.

We didn't have the money to help Lloyd travel overseas. We had to borrow funds from friends, which was far from easy in those days, but we succeeded in getting enough to help him start his journey.

At a travel agency, an agent, upon learning that Lloyd needed a ticket on a steamer sailing to the Soviet Union, frowned. "Mrs. Glascoe, you're really letting your son go to that country?" the agent said.

The agent's comment left me searching for words. Lloyd said heatedly, "I'm not able to find work in the land in which I was born and for which my father died. But in Soviet Russia, they've got work for me."

"Have you tried going from house to house offering your services? You're better off whitewashing cellars in America than working as a top artist in Soviet Russia. Don't you know that those Bolsheviks don't believe in God or the devil?"

"Lloyd is still so young," I said. "I want him to go to Russia and see for himself what life is like there."

Finally, after we dealt with all of the roadblocks, Lloyd was on his way. I cried and cried after I saw him off. I thought, *Who knows what awaits him in that strange country. Will I ever see my son again?*

After Lloyd's departure, I left Westfield, where I had no connections, and moved back to New York, settling in with the Pattersons. Sarah Patterson and I both looked for work. Finally, after an exhausting search, we found jobs in a laundry.

One night, on our way home, we stumbled across a rally outside. We were so tired that we could hardly stand, but we lingered and listened to the speakers. We had found ourselves in the midst of a Communist gathering, and for the first time, I heard ideas that touched me to my core. Suddenly, energy electrified me.

From then on, I attended rallies. I asked a lot of questions of the speakers, who were always happy to answer them. I found that we agreed on things, I told Ella, a coworker at the laundry.

"Margaret," she said, "you'd better keep away from those people. They're all Reds."

This wasn't the first time I'd heard about "Reds." People always said the term with disgust. Now that I was getting to know these "Reds," however, I could clearly see that the press was slandering them.

I'd joined the National Association for the Advancement of Colored People while living in Westfield. There I'd met Mrs. Graves, a black woman who headed the Colored Republican Club. Whenever I offered to host an event, she'd usually say, "Okay, I'll talk to Mr. Johnston about it."

Mr. Johnston was white and served as the head of the Westfield Republican Club.

Once, I needed to see him on the eve of the municipal elections. Our club represented a lot of voters, and the Republican Party wanted to draw us in. I told him that we'd be willing to support the Republican candidates if they'd promise that the municipal authorities would respond better to the needs of the Negro population. Mr. Johnston looked earnestly at me and said, "Mrs. Glascoe, I'm not ready to tell you what we can do, but I urge you to apply all your energy and efforts to get the vote out among your people for the Republican Party. We have a healthy budget, and you'll get what you're due. Just ask Mrs. Graves if we failed to come through for her after the election."

Many who headed our club were cut from the same cloth as Mrs. Graves; but the Reds were different. They truly wanted to help me and others like me. They wanted to teach us how to escape from the endless cycle of poverty.

So, I said to Ella, "If they're Red, then I've been Red all my life but didn't know it."

Sarah Patterson and I had been living in cramped quarters, so Ella had invited me to move in with her. We'd been friends for many years, but since I'd been getting closer with the "Reds," she started distancing herself from me as if suddenly I had an infection. I tried to ignore this. I found what I had spent years looking for, and I threw myself into it with all my heart. I knew I was on the right path, the only path.

A few months later, I finally got a brief letter from Lloyd.

He wrote, "Remember Mom how I couldn't land a job when I got back from college, even though I was hungry for work? Now, I'm on the path you and I have been seeking for so long. I want you to come here too. You'll start a new life here."

I didn't miss a single meeting, not a single rally. Each time, I dragged Ella with me, but the Reds really frightened her. I'd bring the *Daily Worker* home. Ella worried that the neighbors might see the newspaper lying about the place. She'd always try to stash it out of sight; but then, in light of some of our discussions, she started reading it. Just the same, I couldn't convert her to my new faith, and she hated it when my Red comrades started visiting me. In general, she hated white people, just as I had for many years.

My comrades told me to get closer to my laundry coworkers and get them involved in unionizing. This wasn't easy. We'd gone on strike at the laundry recently, which ended in our defeat. The women I worked with were depressed and extremely dubious about any attempts to organize. I talked to them, told them why banding together was important. But they just listened in silence. I couldn't break through their apathy.

Then, the Workers' Center that I'd joined organized a rally to support the Scottsboro Boys.[31] I took some fliers promoting the rally to work and passed them out to my coworkers, all women; but our boss saw me doing this and ran up and grabbed one of the fliers out of my hand.

"What is this?"

"This is a sermon for our church," I said.

He didn't bother reading the handout and just gave it back. So, I succeeded in distributing the fliers, but not a single one of my coworkers showed up at the rally. My encounter with the boss scared them, and, moreover, they'd heard that the Reds were involved in the goings-on with the Scottsboro Boys.

I kept distributing the *Daily Worker* and other Communist materials, but by this point, Ella had stopped letting me bring any of it into our home. So, I'd stash it all at Sarah Patterson's apartment. Then Ella started complaining about my white comrades dropping by. Finally, she told me that I needed to move out. I moved back in with Sarah.

Despite my failed attempt to inspire coworkers to rally, I kept trying to get them to see and feel the same electrifying light that had changed my perception of my future. I tried to change their minds by changing my strategy. Our club held a dance, and I sold some cheap tickets at work. Some of the women who'd bought a ticket decided to skip the event once they found out the Reds were behind it; but the others came and had a good time.

Before long, I had to cease my involvement in this work, but I'd already seen results. Before, blacks and whites in our club, both male and female, weren't comfortable mingling and they even openly avoided each other; now, quite a few of them were club regulars and would dance with each other and eat at the same tables. This happened on its own.

Just like a black man, if a white worker couldn't pay the rent, he was thrown out into the street. If you looked at the soup lines in those days, you'd see white workers standing right beside black workers. Back then, I didn't fully under-stand what it all signified, but now I know how class solidarity among the workers surpasses racial discomfort. I attribute our club's success to this.

> *Reds!*
>
> *Just saying "Red!" out loud in today's America is enough to unleash a new round of frenzied persecution and outrageous slander against the best and the brightest.*
>
> *I hear the pounding of jackboots. It's from the thugs dressed up like Hitler's storm troopers marching along the streets shouting, "We're celebrating Kennedy's assassination! Now it's time to take on the Reds!"*
>
> *America!*
>
> *The cadaverous venom of racism has soaked through your clothes, and sick spots have appeared on your tanned skin.*
>
> *Come to your senses before it's too late, and cast off this poisonous shell of sanctimonious hypocrisy and racial intolerance!*
>
> *Russia—this is you,*
> *you are humane.*
> *Salvatore*[32]

My son discovered a new homeland. Lloyd was so happy that he said the same thing over and over in his letters to me. In his ecstatic words, I'd always find ever more fresh nuances. This country that had adopted him began to seem like some earthly paradise. I would dream about it in my sleep and think about it when awake.

Lloyd became more and more insistent in summoning me to join him. He'd married a Russian girl, and now I had a grandson. More than three years had passed since we'd parted, and my longing to see Lloyd, my new daughter, and my grandson consumed me.[33]

I asked my comrades and the organization to help me, and they promised they would. Often, a lawyer who was also a

Communist came to the club. He heard me out once and said, "You'll get to go. I'll handle it myself."

So, I found myself on the deck of a steamer sailing from New York. I'd found some companions. Ellen Wright, a black woman with two children, was on her way to South Africa to visit her husband, who was participating in an American research expedition. We hardly interacted with the other passengers. On the ship, we experienced the same racial intolerance that prevailed across the USA.

My journey from New York to London went well, all in all, and the next morning, I boarded a Soviet steamship. A different mood altogether existed on this vessel. As I waited to be shown to my cabin, I looked around. A girl passenger looked at me, smiled, and asked, "Do you need any help?"

"No, thank you," I replied. "I think they'll show me to my cabin soon."

"But you don't know any Russian. I'd like to help you."

She stayed by my side until I made it to my cabin. Then, she took it upon herself to look over me.

Immediately, I grew attached to this sweet girl. Deep inside, I fostered the hope that my daughter-in-law would be like her, this Emma from Leningrad.

Upon our arrival in Leningrad, we parted ways. I then took a train to Moscow. Anxiously, at the station, I looked for my son.[34] When I spotted him, I burst into tears—tears of joy. How different he was from the Lloyd, who, in worn-out boots and a shabby jacket, would seek work from dawn to dusk all over Westfield! The smiling man before me was calm, confident, and well dressed; but the self-esteem written all over his face and exuding from his every movement instilled the greatest joy in me. This country was working wonders. Lloyd had found himself here.

If only I'd lived here when I was fighting so hard to raise my son, I wouldn't be such an old woman at the age of forty-three.[35] Now, though, in the USSR, I was growing younger by the day. Often, I visited a black woman friend who'd long ago moved here. Her husband, Mike, who was fluent in Russian, had been working at a Moscow plant for many years. He put everything into his job and was just as passionate about educating himself on various topics. He read books on politics, economics, and philosophy. Often, he'd be up late.

Once, after we all returned to their home late from the theater, my friend and I lay down to sleep. After a few hours, I woke up to find that Mike had covered the lamp with a newspaper and sat at a table scribbling something.

I said, "For heaven's sake, Mike, go to bed. What on earth are you working on at all hours of the night?"

"I'm sorry if I woke you up, Margaret. I have to finish this—it's urgent. We're not fulfilling the plan at work."

I didn't know what he was talking about.

"But, Mike," I said, "can't work wait until morning? You've got to take care of yourself. The plant won't shut down if you wait until tomorrow."

"Do you know what you're saying, Margaret?"

Fully awake now, I rose up and took a seat. Mike went on, "Do you get what it's all about? I'm working for myself. Maybe it's beyond you."

He laughed, seeing me flush with anger.

Mike wasn't the only one with that mindset. I spoke with a lot of workers. "Our five-year plan … our country … our factory …" You had to hear how they sounded when they spoke like that.

After I'd been in Russia for a few months, I truly understood what socialism was. All my life, I'd dreamed of learning a real craft. So, now the time had come to select a field. For some time, I couldn't settle on anything specific. Finally, I started working at an automobile factory.

Thank you, Komsomol girls of the 1930s, the same age as my mother: Raya Kromina—a friendly girl with soft eyes, and shy Klava Gavrilova, and always equally poised, patient, and attentive Zoya Bryantseva, who, along with my dark-faced grandmother, Margaret, knew May Day songs and guided her in her first timid steps at the factory.

Where are you now, white-haired Leila from the electric motor maintenance workshop at the Likhachev Automobile Plant, who so steadfastly helped her with her Russian grammar? Perhaps you had to don a military coat back in the day and the ensuing hardships you endured made your hair go white?

The regular correspondence with family and friends back in America forced me to again experience all that I'd left behind since arriving in the USSR.

The club you organized is doing great, wrote Dora Wormly, my friend from Westfield. *Recently, we helped out the family of a black worker, Stone, who their landlord was trying to evict from their apartment. Stone was out of work for a long time, and his wife only worked two days a week. But he was told he didn't qualify for unemployment since his wife had a job. And so the landlord threw Stone and his wife and young children out onto the street for not making their rent payment. That was when our club members went into action to help them out. We banded together to get his family back into their home. A policeman showed up in response to the ruckus, but the workers disarmed him and tossed him out of the window. The only reason he wasn't hurt was because the apartment was on the ground floor. And so, Mrs. Glascoe, it was a real war, justice prevailed.*

The next day, the following item was in the paper: "In the melee yesterday with the police, the Blacks and Whites were so intermingled that it was hard to tell them apart." Our club is under surveillance. The police are looking for any pretext to shut it down ...

Hugh Patterson wrote as follows:

We all really enjoyed reading your description of the May Day demonstration in Moscow. What a spectacle! I hope that I get to see something like that in America before I die. We're all eager to hear about what you think about life in Soviet Russia, as well.

In Moscow, I got a letter from Ellen, my companion on the steamer that had sailed from New York:

How do you like Soviet Russia? What's it like? Write back and let me know if it's true what they say in the newspapers in America, which is that they take the children away from their parents and don't allow anyone to go to church. How do people treat you there in Soviet Russia? Is there racial intolerance and prejudice there?

Having lived in the Soviet Union for two years, I'd grown accustomed to my independence. I'd become a new person. I looked back at my path in life before this, and I felt like the sacrifices along the way had not been in vain. I'd given my all to my son, who, I felt sure would be a true fighter for socialism.

Chapter 10

In the Land of My Youth

Margaret Glascoe!

You raised a fine son. When he first stepped onto Soviet soil, America was rife with hunger and lynching, the masses of the unemployed were running rampant around a battered country, and Siqueiros's fresco entitled **Street Meeting** *was destroyed simply because it depicted black and white workers next to each other.*

The brown cloud of fascism, nourished by the bourgeoisie, loomed over the horizon, darkening the sky.

The war brought with it unbearable grief. I lost my father. When war broke out, my family and I were evacuated, except for my father, who, as an employee at Radiocomitet, stayed behind in Moscow. One night, a bomb blast left him seriously shell-shocked. He didn't last long after that. He wasn't yet thirty-two years old.[36]

I still remember his kindness and gentleness. I see him sitting in a T-shirt that revealed his strong, dark shoulders, his curly head bent over his typewriter.

From the time I was a toddler, I was used to the rhythmic tap-tap of my father's typewriter and the brushes, paints, and sketches from my mother's artwork. I also had a penchant for drawing from a young age, and in the morning, as soon as I got up, I'd spread out a sheet of Whatman paper. Clutching a thick brush in my left hand—like my father, I was left-handed—I'd draw. I never used pencils, preferring to paint with a brush, constantly dipping it into jars of multicolored gouache paint. My mother thought that my drawings resembled the contemporary Western painting style Tachisme.

A lot of time has passed since then. I've reached adulthood, stepping across the boundary separating me from my childhood and into my independent life. I've tried to imagine how my life would have played out had I been born in America, where, under current laws in some thirty states, my parents could have served years behind bars for the simple reason that my father was black and my mother is white.

I don my raincoat and walk outside onto Prospect Mir. I walk and inhale lungfuls of air. I smile at the people I meet, and they smile back.[37]

Later, I pass through the bloody, smoky fields of Georgia and Mississippi. I am following in the footsteps of James Meredith as he boldly steps across the threshold of Oxford University.[38] *I follow in the footsteps of seventeen-year-old Hazel Ruth Adams, who pays no attention to the boycott they announce to me. I sit down behind a desk at the "white" college of the state of Virginia, and I find a hail of stone and tear gas bombs lobbed at me from the unrestrained Ku Klux Klansmen of Alabama.*

I recognize a long-legged, laughing fellow holding a banjo. It's Pete Seeger, a talented collector and performer of folk songs. He sings, and the exuberance of the melody captures me. It is as if my second sight. It's as if I see the Kentucky miners who have their own motto: "Hold on to each other more tightly."

I see the Indians of the town of Maxton facing the persecution of the Ku Klux Klan.[39]

"You sounded great tonight, Pete," I tell him.

"Thanks!" he says.

I listen to the volcanic beating of the wounded heart of Africa and, having brushed up against immortality, I bow my head to the proud, heroic lives of Iraqis as they struggle to shake off the shackles of colonialism.

I shake hands with Manolis Glezos and move on.[40]

I stride along Prospect Mir, forging ahead into the future.

Lloyd Patterson's Last Letter to His Family

Note from James Patterson:

This is the content of a typed version, provenance unknown, of a handwritten letter from my father. He tried in every possible way to conceal it, but he suffered a serious concussion after a bombing in Moscow. The words jumped, not obeyed. He was very sick and didn't remember everything correctly.

> January 13, 1942
>   Dear Vera!
>   I am writing this letter from Khabarovsk.
>   We arrived this morning. It is very cold here, more than 35 degrees but the Khabarovsk people do not consider it very cold. Goncharov and Zhukov are already at our new place of work. We had a nice trip on the train, our couple [*sic*] was a little damp but it was all right. An unpleasant thing happened at the very end of the trip. We forgot the typewriter on the train. That upset all of us very much but we will send a telegram to the nearest station and tell them to send it back to Khabarovsk where it will be forwarded to us. We will leave on the 7 o'clock train this evening and will be in Komsomolsk tomorrow at 2 o'clock in the day.
>   Khabarovsk is much smaller than I thought. Its population is only about 200,000. It has one main street

named Karl Marx. Stanley, another lady comrade—I always forget her name—and I took a walk in some of the stores.[1] I bought Jimmy a pair of brown low shoes (size 33) and Junior (size 30), both shoes are with rubbers. But I don't know how I will ever get them to you. However I will put them in my suitcase until I know of someone who is going to Sverdlovsk. Or maybe I'll keep them. They will always come in good use. If they get too small for Jimmy then Junior and Tommy can wear them.

Please write and tell me about the wood. Did you find a place to put it? Did any of it get stolen? Did grandfather cut it up for you?[2] I don't know why but I don't think there was four meters of wood, but less. However I hope it will be enough for the entire winter, so I wouldn't have to worry about my family.

A little while ago we listened to the American broadcast. It was the first time I had listened to our broadcast. I heard Burroughs and Ruth speaking.

Stanley sends her best regards to you all. Soon we will begin working. I am very anxious to start work because I am tired of traveling and want to get busy.

Write to me at Komsomolsk.

I think it will take a letter 3 weeks to get here from Sverdlovsk. Please write regularly and let me know how the family is getting along. And if there has been any reaction at the Radio Committee to my telegram. When I get to Komsomolsk I will take care of the apartment, payment and the piano.

I do not know just when I will be able to send you any money. I understand that sometimes there is a very long hold-up in money here, so you must be economical with the money you receive from the Radio Committee in Sverdlovsk. And then when I do send the money I will send it by mail because there is no photo-telegraph in Komsomolsk.

Well, be a good girl and don't forget me. I hope that someday soon we will be lock [*sic*] together—our whole family together.

Many kisses to you all,
Your Lloyd

[1] Ann Stanley was born in Riga in 1904. Her revolutionary parents immigrated to the United States two years later. Stanley joined the Communist Party in 1925 and married an American, who was sent to Moscow to attend the Lenin Institute. She joined her husband in 1932 and worked as a journalist. Her husband died in 1941, and she went to Komsomolsk, where she worked in broadcasting with Lloyd Patterson.
[2] At that time, Vera Aralova's mother was the only grandparent with the family.

The Pattersons:
Expatriate and Native Son

by Rimgaila Salys

During the early 1930s, an unknown number of black Americans traveled to the Union of Soviet Socialist Republics to escape racist persecution and the economic hardships of the Great Depression. Other black sojourners simply wanted to see and understand the great socialist experiment for themselves.[41] Among those who settled permanently in the land of the Soviets was Lloyd Walton Patterson, who pursued a successful career as a designer, lecturer, and radio announcer until his untimely death during World War II. His son James gained even greater renown as a child actor and later as Soviet Russia's native-born black poet. While Lloyd willingly served as an icon of racial tolerance in the USSR during the thirties, James initially played a similar role, albeit not always happily; but ultimately, he found a felicitous compromise in representing Soviet racial tolerance abroad, primarily to African countries. While his father's construction of self in the USSR was mainly determined by ideological commitment, James's more complicated negotiation of identity was predicated not only on ideology but also encompassed a cinematic persona, the career of Socialist Realist poet, and a concomitant personal identification with Aleksandr Pushkin, Russia's national poet.[42]

The Father

Был отец и строен, и подтянут,
В полушубке белом, как сугроб.

Father was both slender and smart-looking
In a sheepskin jacket as white as a snowdrift.

James Patterson, "Detstvo"["Childhood"]

Lloyd Patterson (1910-1942), the son of Margaret Glascoe and her first husband, Archie Patterson, was born on 165th Street in the Bronx. Years later, he, his mother and her second husband, Steve Glascoe, moved to Westfield, New Jersey, where Lloyd would attend high school. When he was required to repeat one year of classes because of poor grades, he began talking about dropping out and looking for a job. Terrified about his future, Margaret mortgaged her house and sent Lloyd to Hampton Institute, in Virginia, where he did well, majoring in interior decorating although he did not graduate.[43] As a black man looking for work during the Depression, Lloyd found only odd jobs, such as house painting: "At that time the Lichtman movie chain had given the contract for redecorating a motion picture house of its chain in Hampton. Mr. Patterson said that he applied for work with the decorators, but was turned down because the decorators had an air-tight Jim Crow union."[44]

In 1932, Lloyd answered a newspaper advertisement inviting black actors to participate in the *Black and White* film project, commissioned by the Comintern, an organization promoting world communism, and Rote Hilfe, a support organization for imprisoned Communists. According to the script, the film was to depict racism and labor conflict at a steel mill in Birmingham, Alabama. It was to be shot in Moscow at Mezhrabpomfil'm Studio; the Comintern would reimburse participants' travel and living expenses. On April 7, 1932, African-American social activist Louise Thompson accepted Lloyd into the group, which included Langston Hughes as consultant. [45] Lloyd, who had been struggling with economic and racial burdens during the Depression, paid his own way to Moscow, a testament to his commitment to social change and the desire to see for himself the Soviet promise of a better society. The group of twenty-one blacks of different backgrounds and one white reached Moscow on June 26, 1932, received a warm welcome, traveled, enjoyed themselves, but were given little work. Several months later, foreign policy considerations led to the cancellation of the project: The Soviets preferred not to irritate the US with a film on American racism prior to expected diplomatic recognition of the Soviet Union. [46] For African-American intellectuals, the trip was important as evidence of an international antiracist movement that supported their struggle for equality in the US. In the end, three members of the group decided to remain in Russia: Wayland Rudd, who was to become the most prominent black stage and screen actor of the Stalin era; the journalist and post office operations specialist, Homer Smith; and the paperhanger, Lloyd Patterson, as he was identified on Louise Thompson's list. [47]

Lloyd had joined the Communist Youth League [*Komsomol*] before leaving the US and apparently felt at home in the Soviet Union, perceiving the country as free of racism and feeling energized by the optimism and promise of the new socialist society: "Mother, life out here is simply bubbling over like the water in a tea kettle. There is so much work here that there is a lack of workers. They don't even notice that I am black here. Only sometimes children meeting me in the street cry—not spitefully but only with surprise: Oh! Look how black he is. Leave everything and come to the Soviet Union." [48] She did: Margaret Glascoe arrived there on June 10, 1934, became a shock worker in the electrical repairs shop of the Stalin

Automobile Factory, and was recommended for study at the Markhlevskii Communist University of National Minorities of the West.[49]

Several months after his arrival in Russia, Lloyd married Vera Ippolitovna Aralova (1911-2001), whom he had met either at a party given by Aralova's friend Lili Brik or at the Meyerkhol'd Theatre when the young theatre artist and painter translated for him during a production of Mayakovsky's *The Bathhouse.* [50] Soon, Lloyd found interior decorating work painting the gold and silver leaf decorations for a ninety-room addition to the Hotel Metropole. He also worked with his wife designing portable sets for the Central Collective Farm Theatre, and the couple received the prestigious assignment of decorating Kuznetskii Most with life-size satirical figures for May Day 1933.[51] Lloyd also did set design for Mezhrabpom-fil'm and later became a member of the central committee of MOPR [International Organization for Aid to Revolutionary Fighters], giving speeches in cities and at construction sites about the predicament of blacks in the US. Over the course of several years, he and his wife would have three children: James (b. 1933),[52] Lloyd Junior (called "Dzhun'" or "Dzhun'ka," 1935-1960), killed in an automobile accident in Moscow, and Tom (b. 1937), formerly a cameraman at Ostankino and now retired.

In 1935, Lloyd, along with black Muscovites Wayland Rudd, Homer Smith, John Goode, Coretti Arle-Titz, and several others, was a member of an informal black group organized by Lovett Fort-Whiteman. The Soviet authorities perceived this group as anti-Party because of its emphasis on race rather than class, and the existence of the group contributed to Fort-Whiteman's arrest in 1937. During the 1930s, Lloyd had collected material for a planned history of the Negro in the United States;[53] he may therefore have shared Fort-Whiteman's emphasis on maintaining race consciousness, even in officially colorblind Soviet society. In 1936, he played George, the pastor's runaway slave, in an adaptation of *Tom Sawyer* (dir. Lazar' Frenkel' and Gleb Zatvornitskii, Ukrainfil'm) and in 1938 became a writer and announcer for the All-Union Radio Committee [*Vsesoiuznyi komitet po radiofikatsii i radioveshchaniiu pri Sovete narodnykh komissarov*].[54]

The black actress and social activist Frances E. Williams, who was studying drama at the Meyerkhol'd and Vakhtangov theatres, lived with the Pattersons from 1934 to 1936, helping with cooking and childcare. She has left an oral account that gives a sense of their lives during these years:

Q: We were talking about Lloyd Patterson.
A: [...] Lloyd worked all over the country. I remember when the Scottsboro boys—Remember when we had the big campaign here for the Scottsboro boys? And when they made it a kind of international thing, Lloyd was going all over the Soviet Union making speeches about the eight little Scottsboro boys, and I remember I was living with him at that time, and he came home to tell us what had happened at the last meeting, and this meeting this night he was talking about the eight little Scottsboro boys, and the woman who was interpreting for him or translating for him said, she started crying so she could hardly translate what he was saying [...]. Lloyd came home that night and he was telling us about this woman who had cried so and said that she was translating and instead of saying the eight little Scottsboro boys she said the eight-year old Scottsboro boy, and he got so amused at that, and the people took him up and threw him up in the air and caught him, and they threw him up in the air and caught him, and he pissed in his pants all down the back, and he came home with this overcoat covering him. I'll never forget that night. [...] But they were a wonderful family. He was a very conscientious dedicated person and a beautiful young man. They had two sons—young Jim and I don't know the youngest son's name, I should know but I've forgotten it. But at that time I

learned much of my Russian teaching them Russian, and then I would do much of the marketing, and I had to learn Russian if I went to the market. So that was fun, and I lived—as I told you the other day—Irvine Levin[55] had offered me this very fine apartment when no one could get an apartment, and that was the other, it was a beef that I had with Patterson, because he didn't really want me to have that apartment, and I didn't take it because I met Vera at the M[e]yerhold Theatre where I studied, and she was the set designer and costume designer and very fine artist, and invited me to move in with them. They had two rooms in a very new apartment, where you had a communal kitchen and bath, and you had two good-sized rooms, and one was the bedroom for their family—Lloyd and Vera and young Jim—and then they had a baby that was quite young, about a year old, and Vera's brother who was then getting his masters, and he was also learning how to fly a gyroplane, play a violin, and what was funny—I had one corner in the room. Then they rented out corners you see I had a corner, each one had their own corner, so that if you had a big room, you could rent out four corners. [...]

Q. What was your first impression of Lloyd Patterson?

A: He was warm and charming and beautiful. He was chocolate brown with sparkling eyes and well-shaped narrow head, and always anxious to help. He was very warm, and he and Vera were very good together. [...] Lloyd also played the piano and sang, and while I was at their home living, the trade union sent in people to see how people were living, their people were living, what their needs were, what should be in the home that was not there. Can you imagine that happening in the United States? But there I remember one day I was the only one at home, and this woman came to the door and told me who she was and what she wanted, and she said did I have, could she see any paintings that Vera had done. There at that time paper was very scarce. Anything Vera could paint on she painted on; I don't care whether it was a piece of a cardboard box. I just can't tell you the pieces of material that Vera painted on; there was such a wide variety of just everything that had a surface. And I'll never forget going into the closet and getting out all these various kinds of shapes and pieces and textured materials to bring in for this woman to see that Vera had done all these paintings on, and she was so impressed, and then I told her about Lloyd and how he could play and sing and how wonderful he was, and some of the things he sang and places where he had been singing, and you know what happened? They sent in, they said if these people have this much talent and have this much to give, they need a helper in the house so that they will have more time to get this accomplished. Isn't that beautiful? I was so impressed I cannot tell you, and they did send in a housekeeper, we had a difficult time getting the right one, but we did have some household help then, which made it much easier for all of us. [...]

Q: Did Lloyd and Vera encounter any problems of racism?

A: Oh I doubt that very much. I think it would be just the opposite, that's the beautiful thing. You see people were so grateful for anything that made life better for them, and Lloyd being there and Vera and being in the M[e]yerhold Theatre and artist and Lloyd singing and playing and a happy family, and of course his work was mostly political work, I think, but he was such a beautiful person that he would add to any place he happened to be.[56]

On July 28, 1941, Vera and the children were evacuated to Kashino, near Sverdlovsk, along with the families of other radio workers, and the children were placed in a boarding school.[57] Lloyd remained in Moscow and in October suffered a concussion from a nearby bomb explosion; but soon he returned to work and was assigned to a new branch of state radio, broadcasting to the US, Great Britain, and China from Komsomol'sk. On his way there, he spent a few days with his family in Sverdlovsk. Eight-year-old James remembered that his father felt lightheaded and unwell but tried to hide his condition from the family; this was to be their last meeting. In 1942, Lloyd lost consciousness during a radio broadcast and was taken to a military hospital, where he died on March 9.[58] His grave has never been located, apparently because he was buried in the Komsomol'sk city cemetery located on the Northern Highway. In the 1960s, the cemetery was destroyed during excavations for a reinforced concrete factory erected on the site.[59] A plaque on the former state radio building in Komsomol'sk, requested by his wife, remains his sole memorial.[60]

As a young black man growing up in Depression-era America, Lloyd Patterson was unusual in the will and energy with which he became the agent of his own fate. Unquestionably, his decision to settle in the USSR allowed him to develop his talents and fulfill his potential in a way that was impossible in the US of the 1930s. Lloyd and Vera, daughter of a scout in Budennyi's cavalry and herself a successful theatre artist, were a poster couple for the Soviet government's policy of racial tolerance, and grown-up James Patterson became Soviet Russia's black poet. Foreign-born blacks and their children, along with leftist visitors like Paul Robeson and Langston Hughes, modeled the ideology of Soviet racial tolerance, which permitted the association of Russianness with whiteness to continue as before and essentially elided the presence of a long-time, native-born black population, the Abkhazian blacks.[61]

The Son

James Patterson was part of the second generation that succeeded the 1930s black émigrés to the USSR. He was born in Russia, with Russian as his native language, and faced a different process of integration into Russian society than did his father. Aleksei Balabanov, not known for tolerance, frames the issue succinctly in the 2005 film *Zhmurki* [*Dead Man's Bluff*] in which one of a trio of bumbling gangsters is a black Russian. The mocking question his white partners in crime address to him becomes an insistent refrain in the film: *"—Ty negr?"* to which he always answers: *"Ia russkii!"* [—Are you a Negro? —I'm Russian!]. As a black Russian, James negotiated identity during the Soviet era in three interrelated ways: through his cinematic persona; by the practice of Socialist Realism, both as a literary mode and in its ideological orientations during the late Soviet era; and through a multifaceted self-identification with his ideal and man for all seasons, Aleksandr Pushkin.

Born July 17, 1933, James is the oldest son of Lloyd Patterson. Before World War II, he studied the cello and piano at the Gnesin School, but the outbreak of the war and the family's evacuation to the Urals interrupted his schooling. Vera and the boys returned to Moscow on October 12, 1943.[62] Apart from her theatre and film work and individual commissions, Vera embarked on a successful career as a representative of the *Khudozhestvennyi fond* [Art Fund], the social support and business arm of the Union of Russian Artists, established in 1940, which sold artists' works and handled commissions from state organizations and enterprises. In the late fifties, Vera, the chief designer for one of the departments at *Dom mody* [House of Fashion], headed up an exhibition of Russian fashion in Paris. Her handmade women's boots with an appliqué heel were a sensation at the exhibition and widely copied by European firms, but they brought her no money. Upon the initiative of Yekaterina Furtseva, minister of culture, Vera was later awarded the rank of *Zasluzhennyi khudozhnik RSFSR* [Honored Artist of the RSFSR].[63]

With three boys to support in the difficult postwar years, Vera first tried to place James, who didn't even know how to swim, in the Leningrad Nakhimov Naval School.[64] Initially, he was accepted, but then he was excluded because he had lost a year of school during the war and was older than other students in his cohort. At the same time, students were being selected in Leningrad for the newly organized Nakhimov Naval School in Riga, where James was accepted in 1945.[65] Subsequently, he graduated from officers' school in Leningrad (1955) and served as a submarine officer. His years at the Riga naval school were apparently a happy time and, encouraged by a teacher, he began writing poetry there. Although James was placed in the school out of necessity, his love for the sea appears in much of his poetry, and half of the collection *Zaliv dobrogo nachala* [*The Bay of Good Beginning*, 1984][66] consists of marine poems and verse relating to school friends:

Подросткам, из штанишков выросшим,
Нам флот, как отец, помогал.
И кто-то из нас был нахимовцем,
А ныне уже адмирал!
Знакома нам детская тактика
И прозвищ шутливых укол.
Но видно, от прозвища Африка
Я все ж недалеко ушел…
Мы эти бокалы поднимем,
Смеясь и немного грустя,
И снова друг друга обнимем
Еще четверть века спустя.

Like a father, our fleet
Helped adolescents grown out of short pants.
And one of us was a Nakhimov student,
And now is already an admiral!
We're familiar with children's tactics
And the humorous pinprick of nicknames.
But it seems that I haven't gone far
From the nickname "Africa" …
We'll raise these glasses,

Laughing and a little sad,
And we'll hug each other again
In another quarter century.

"Тринадцатое сентября 1980 года"
["The Thirteenth of September," 1980]

These lines suggest that while James felt the sting of his nickname, "Africa," he nevertheless made many friends in the navy with whom he maintained contact over the years. One incident of racial prejudice is recorded in a classmate's memoir from the Leningrad Officers' School: One night, the officer on duty was making rounds and noticed that a cadet was sleeping with his foot sticking out of the blanket. The officer asked his assistant why the cadet hadn't washed his feet. Hesitantly, the assistant tried to explain that this was a "Negro," but the officer responded, "Well, all the same, make him go and wash them!"[67] Though an average student, James was the most prominent cadet of the Riga naval school because of his iconic childhood role as little Jimmy in Grigorii Aleksandrov's *Circus*. In a widely publicized event, the film's main star, Liubov' Orlova, and Aleksandrov visited him at the school in 1949 when they were shooting *Vstrecha na El'be* [*Meeting on the Elbe*] in Riga. Later, James read his poetry at Orlova's concerts in various parts of the country. The actress called him her *kino-syn* [film-son] and maintained friendly relations with the family until her death in 1975.[68]

While still a navy lieutenant, James enrolled in the Gorky Literature Institute in 1957 and graduated in 1962.[69] He became a Party member in 1960 and a member of the Writers' Union in 1967, recommended by the poet Mikhail Svetlov. During his career in Russia, he published seven collections of verse and two books of family and autobiographical memoirs.[70]

James was Vera Aralova's favorite child, and she kept him close throughout her life.[71] He married late, toward the end of the 1980s, but his mother never approved of his young wife, Irina Tolokonnikova, a teacher from the Urals city of Zlatoust. Vera considered her too ordinary for the elite Moscow circles in which she and her son moved. James traveled back and forth between his mother's Moscow residence and his wife's apartment in Zvenigorod.[72] The couple divorced in 1994 before James's departure to the US.

Like many Russians—and especially former establishment intellectuals—James found it impossible to earn a living during the economic crises of the early 1990s, and his mother had few clients for her paintings. For some time, they survived on their pensions and by renting out their Moscow apartment, but eventually mother and son moved together to the US. In 1995, they settled in Washington, DC, where they had American relatives who helped them get established. For a time, they eked out a living by selling Vera's paintings— mostly copies of her earlier works—and James, unsuccessfully, tried acting and attempted to find a publisher for his verse. Vera died in September 2001. Without his mother, James gradually turned inward, lost touch with friends, fell ill, and apparently was again helped by his American relatives. In 2011, he collapsed and was hospitalized for more than a year. For his eightieth birthday, the Russian ambassador and embassy employees visited James, bearing gifts. He suffered a stroke in 2014.[73]

Cinematic Racial Myth Then and Now

In his role as little Jimmy in *Circus*, James embodied the cinematic ideal of racial tolerance officially propagated under High Stalinism. Nevertheless, from the 1930s to the present, Russian cultural discourse has displayed a tension regarding the representation of black Russians as fraternal other and fellow citizen. Whether expatriates or native sons, Soviet blacks were in constant negotiation with Russianness, claiming inclusion while seeking elusive authenticity. This fraught cinematic myth of racial tolerance, sourced in little Jimmy, continues to resonate in post-Soviet space and merits elaboration in the following two sections.

Grigorii Aleksandrov's *Circus* (1936) was one of the most popular films of High Stalinism. It pleased both the authorities and Russian audiences, successfully combining ideology with entertainment, comedy with spectacle. It made three-year-old Jimmy Patterson famous. The film tells the story of Marion Dixon, a white American circus star performing in Moscow who falls in love with a Russian performer who introduces her to the values of Soviet society. Kneishitz, Dixon's jealous manager, tries to ruin her by revealing her secret: She is the biological mother of an illegitimate child whose father is black. The circus audience, however, welcomes the little boy without prejudice, and Dixon remains in Russia, marching in the May Day parade on Red Square.

Internationalism had been official policy since Lenin's time, and the new 1936 constitution guaranteed equal rights to all citizens, irrespective of nationality and race, as well as equal rights for women, with provisions for maternity leave and better social services for children. The circus lullaby episode—Jimmy's acceptance into the Soviet community of peoples—established what became the Soviet myth of racial tolerance.[74]

In 2009, Valerii Todorovskii released the musical film *Stiliagi* [*Hipsters*], which quotes *Circus* in important ways and demonstrates the continuing presence of the filmic myth of racial tolerance as cemented in national memory and inextricably linked to James Patterson in his little Jimmy role. The film, set in 1955-56 during the Thaw, deals with a cult of jazz-loving dandies who imitate what they think is an American phenomenon and are persecuted by the *Komsomol* and the

KGB. *Komsomolets* Mels (named for Marx, Engels, Lenin, and Stalin) transforms into Mel and marries Polina or Polly, a *stiliaga* girl, and they are going to have a baby. Polly gives birth to a boy of black and white heritage—fathered by a man other than Mel—causing tensions between the couple, but they are eventually reunited in a traditional ending for the musical, as *Hipsters* extends its message of inclusivity and tolerance from the couple to the outside world.[75]

Using a different time frame referencing the fate of multiracial *festival'nye deti* [festival children], conceived during the 1957 Moscow international youth festival, Todorovskii readdresses the message of *Circus*, making a plea for individual and lifestyle—not only racial—tolerance in post-Soviet society in the final unifying spectacle. At the same time, he quotes motifs from *Circus* as the iconic Soviet urban musical: First, ordinary Russian people welcome the biracial baby, modeled on little Jimmy, as "ours," and later there is a quotation of *Circus's* lullaby episode as the baby is passed around among grotesquely fawning *stiliagi* friends until the mother angrily takes him away. By implication, the parodic episode, along with the mother's reaction, rejects the sentimental falseness of the *Circus* lullaby. Handing a startled baby around a crowd of admirers may afford the latter gratification, or in the case of *Circus*, some politically kitsch emotions, but, says Todorovskii, the benefit is to the state, not the baby.

In spite of its explicitly stated message of tolerance, *Circus* projects a different racial discourse from *Hipsters*. Little Jimmy is welcomed into the family of Soviet peoples in the circus finale and then participates in the Red Square parade as a citizen of the Soviet state. Yet the underlying discourse of the film is racist, contradicting the myth of racial tolerance embodied by James Patterson in his cinematic role. Black and white function with their traditional negative/positive valorizations in the film: Marion's black wig denotes her false performative persona, hiding her genuine and virtuous blonde self; the villain Kneishitz is dark-haired and wears a black cloak, while the circus performers march in sport whites in the Red Square parade. This same color scheme infiltrates the comic "cleansing" of Jimmy's face in the metro episode:

—Oh, oh, oh, how black you are!
(Jimmy sticks his tongue out at his rescuer, Skameikin.)
—How dirty I've gotten you! (Skameikin rubs Jimmy's face with a handkerchief.)[76]

Toward the end of *Circus*, when Jimmy runs away from Kneishitz, the little boy is juxtaposed with a dog and then a monkey performing tricks. When the circus director publicly refutes Kneishitz's racist remarks, his comic repartee verges on the vulgar, partly continuing the association of Jimmy with animals: "Have as many [children] as you like—black ones, white ones, red ones, even blue ones, even pink ones with stripes, even dappled ones. Go right ahead!" Although Marion's affair with a black man occurs outside the *Circus* narrative and is not explicitly disparaged, the ideological message of the film is nonetheless that Marion's hypersexuality, as demonstrated by her desire for a black man, has been channeled into a proper and legitimate union with Martynov, the Stalinist New Man, who is white.[77]

In *Hipsters*, the conception of Polly's child with a black man is framed very differently, as she explains to Mel:

—His name was Michael.
—One of ours?
—No, he was an American. He was walking along Sadovaia, trying to stop someone to find out where he was, and people kept running away from him.
—Did you love him?
—No, it was something completely different. Imagine, a person flew in from another planet only for a

few hours. And there's so much to ask about them and so much to tell about us. But the minutes keep ticking away, and soon he must return to his rocket. And we both know that we'll never see each other again.

Polly understands her meeting with the black American as an encounter with a visitor from another planet, as completely outside conventional moral boundaries, a supremely unique event, and therefore almost as a blessing.

The cinematic myth of racial tolerance personified by little Jimmy gave Russians throughout the Soviet era an idealized warm, fuzzy feeling about him and themselves. Now-famous Jimmy Patterson was prominently featured in the 1936 physical culture parade, sitting in a large poppy blossom.[78] A classmate at the Nakhimov School remembers the "*Circus* effect": "James was the indispensable hero of all essays about the school, and artists would even come to draw his portrait."[79] During a Victory Day parade, Stalin recognized James marching with Nakhimov cadets and pointed to him.[80] In 1959, Admiral Ivan Isakov wrote a secret letter to Khrushchev, citing the novelty of a black naval officer like James and proposing the recruitment of hundreds of other black men from the South into the Soviet navy as propaganda against endemic American racism.[81]

In interviews, James Patterson says that he gave poetry readings all over the USSR during the Soviet years. Audiences were appreciative, but they really wanted him to tell stories about the filming of *Circus*, and he got a little tired of it: "People meant well, of course, but at that time, as a man of letters, I really wanted to read my poems."[82] Clearly, to the broader population, even as an adult, he remained in a different category from the African tribesmen, American slaves, and criminals played by Wayland Rudd and Robert Ross in films such as *Velikii uteshitel'* [*The Great Consoler*, 1933], *Tom Sawyer* (1936), *Piatnadtsatiletnii kapitan* [*The Fifteen-Year-Old*

Captain, 1945], *Miklukho-Makhlai* (1948), and *Tainstvennyi ostrov* [*The Mysterious Island*, 1941]. These stereotypical, albeit well-intentioned, depictions of black men, could not compete with the image of the completely lovable little boy of *Circus*. The mystique of "our little Jimmy" always surrounded James Patterson, protected him from everyday racism, and provided him with the opportunity for self-actualization, ultimately facilitating a successful literary career. He occupied a privileged position in the USSR because it was precisely his "otherness," as lovingly adopted by Soviet citizens in the *Circus* finale, that validated official ideology.

The Socialist Realist Poet

Rossiia-Afrika, James Patterson's first poetry collection, came out in 1963 and *Nochnye strekozy* [*Night Dragonflies*], the last, a chapbook of eighteen poems, was published in 1993. Most of his work, in print runs of ten- to fifty-thousand copies, appeared during the Stagnation or late Soviet era, when the liberalizing Thaw had ended, literary experimentation was discouraged, and controls on the arts were tightened. A ten-year gap existed between the first collection and the second, *Rozhdenie livnia*, because James was dissatisfied with the quality of *Rossiia-Afrika*, his diploma project. Subsequently, he produced poetry collections every two to six years through 1984, which marked the end of his regular publication. During the Stagnation Era, James became Russia's black poet and a Socialist Realist establishment figure—another negotiation of identity.

Nevertheless, like the iconic little Jimmy of *Circus*, the poet James Patterson remained a token figure in the literary culture of Developed Socialism. It was Russian cinema of the time that staged the hegemonic model for the Russianness of black characters most transparently. Two very different films commenting on the black man in Russia were released in 1976 during the reactionary Brezhnev era. In *The Magic Circle* [*Vol-*

shebnyi krug, dir. Valentin Kozachkov], a foreign black wrestler named Chembers Peps is obsessed with playing Taras Bul'ba, a Cossack national hero, in a circus pantomime; but the one time he is allowed to play his hero, he does it in whiteface as he strives to be more Russian.[83] In Aleksandr Mitta's *The Tale of How Tsar Peter Married Off His Blackamoor* [*Skaz pro to, kak tsar' Petr arapa zhenil*], loosely based on Pushkin's unfinished historical novel, Vladimir Vysotsky plays Ibragim Gannibal in minimal blackface. Although there were—admittedly less remarkable—black actors available, such as Ermengel'd Konovalov, who had played Ibragim in *Ballada o Beringe i ego druz'iakh* [*The Ballad of Bering and His Friends*, dir. Iurii Shvyrev, 1970], Mitta made a different choice out of necessity but also driven by a patriotic rather than racial agenda:

> In the story of Gannibal we were attracted by the opportunity of expressing the theme of patriotism emotionally, without loud, ostentatious words. [...] Gannibal, the famous "blackamoor of Peter the Great," was in an unusual situation, in which he had to realize his Russian patriotism in a particular way: he became a son of Russia, Peter's son, but he had no family in Russia, no roots in the Russian earth. Our "experiment," if you like, with Gannibal—was an attempt to tell about a pure, unadulterated sense of motherland. [...] Several Ethiopians auditioned for the role of Ibragim. But they had behavioral stereotypes that were completely unfamiliar to us: gestures, ways of walking and speaking. This was exotic and took us away from our task. In addition, Ibragim was essentially Russian. It was important for us to emphasize this. And, since the entire film was something of a masquerade, we decided that it wouldn't really matter that the Negro was played by a Russian actor in makeup. Vysotsky was better than the others in screen tests and we invited him to play the role.[84]

Vysotsky's cult status and enormous moral authority, then at its peak, clearly enhanced the characterization of Gannibal as Peter's only honest and loyal aide in a circle of corrupt courtiers. If Ibragim's assertion, *"Ia russkii!,"* later ironized over and rejected by Balabanov in *Zhmurki*, was crucial to Mitta's figuration of the character as a Russian patriot, then it did not matter to him whether Gannibal was portrayed by a white or black Russian since they were both equally Russian. Mitta struggles with genre and register in this not entirely successful film and, in contradiction of its serious patriotic message, also underscores its comedic-ironic "dress-up" quality as another justification for the use of a white actor. While the moral authority of Vysotsky certainly elevated the depiction of Gannibal in the film, the character as played by a white man in light blackface nevertheless again rehearsed the understanding of Russianness as whiteness among broader Russian audiences.

During the Stagnation Era, James Patterson developed into a middle-rank artist, not a Voznesensky nor a Brodsky. Of the names we still recognize today, the *style* of James's verse could be compared to that of Bulat Okudzhava or Iaroslav Smeliakov—simply stated thoughts and ideas, transparent language, traditional meter and rhyme, sparing use of metaphors, and avoidance of more complex tropes. While Okudzhava's largely apolitical sincerity was perceived as a threat to the system, James was not an artist who questioned Soviet myths or the twentieth century history of Russia. If his father had been transgressive vis-à-vis the country of his birth, its system and practices, the son, by following his idolized father's strong convictions and for his own career reasons, was more conformist, unable or unwilling to question the history or realities of the country of *his* birth. James's introduction to his 1978 collection *Vzaimodeistvie* [*Interaction*] is couched in the conventional language of the time: "I am constantly excited about the phenomenal [*grandioznyi*] progress taking place before our eyes: the strengthening battle of the world working class for its rights, problems of disarmament, as well as the process of decolonization taking place on the African continent. The new poems, written as a result of trips to the majestic construction sites of the five-year plan and to foreign countries that have set out on the path to independent development, form the basis of this collection." By the late seventies, such language was not absolutely necessary, but James abandoned this Party-speak only in the 1984 collection.

His poetry of the Soviet period falls into several thematic categories. As a Socialist Realist poet, he wrote about workers and construction projects. His internationalist commitment, ideologically correct but also sincere, led to poems on American themes, inspired by several trips to the US, and to the larger and more interesting African theme, present in almost every collection. The American poems focus primarily on racism, including his own family's experience, and the national predilection for violence. While his poetry reflects racial prejudice in the US and South Africa, it does not speak of it in Russia.[85] Interestingly, only in one poem ("Iz detstva" ["From Childhood"]) does James allude to Russian women workers' criticism upon seeing Vera Aralova's three black children in Sverdlovsk: "где позже кворум женщин трудовых/ Про маму говорил: иная, дескать,/ своих не любит, как она чужих ..." ["where later a quorum of working women said of Mama: she's different, they said; she doesn't love her own, how could she [love] foreigners ..."].

African themes occupy a special place in James Patterson's oeuvre. With the Thaw, the Soviet focus on racism and colonialism in Africa as aspects of the class struggle gave way to a policy emphasizing the Soviet development model as an alternative to Western capitalism, dissemination of cultural information about the USSR, political and military support for some liberation movements, and an increased number of stipends for Africans to study at the newly founded Lumumba University. "Gradually, Africa moved from the periphery of Soviet foreign policy concerns to the center stage of Cold War politics. ... In Africa, the USSR sought closer relations with the regimes sympathetic to Marxism."[86] James first traveled to Africa in 1969 and made additional trips during the 1970s, visiting Zaire, Tanzania, Zambia, Kenya, Uganda, and other African states as a cultural representative of the Soviet government.[87]

However, his African poems extend beyond the political. In one of his best-known poems, "Daua-Daua," he writes about the beauty of the landscape, people, and animals, the great African artisans, and the African conception of malevolent fortune. He sees the Africans not as victims and objects of compassion, as they were commonly portrayed in the Soviet media, but as agents of their own destiny in achieving progress on the continent. His strongest statement about Africa comes in "Poetu Borisu Kornilovu—avtoru poemy *Moia Afrika*" ["To the Poet Boris Kornilov, the Author of the Long Poem *My Africa*"] in the 1980 *Zimnie lastochki* collection. Kornilov (1907-38), the first husband of Ol'ga Berggol'ts, was a member of the *Smena* group and the author of the lyrics to Shostakovich's "Pesnia o vstrechnom" ["Song of the Counterplan"]. *Moia Afrika* narrates the life of a young ROSTA artist who meets a black Red Army officer on Nevskii Prospect in 1918, then searches for him at the front, and, after learning of the officer's heroic death for the Soviet cause, joins the Red Army with the intention of repaying the symbolic debt: "Как умер он в бою/ за сумрачную,/ За свою Россию,/ Так я умру за Африку мою" ["Just as he died in battle,/ For his own/ For gloomy Russia,/ So I will die for my Africa"]. In his own programmatic statement, James recognizes his allegiance to Russia, but his loyalty to Africa is even stronger:

Живя в условиях добрососедства,
людского пониманья и тепла,
всем существом я ощущал,
что с детства
она меня, Россия, берегла.
Народы голос обретали.
Я, существуя с веком наравне,[88]
не замечал того, что прорастали
ростки грядущей Африки во мне.
И я за честь России постою.
И это будет высшая награда.
Но, несомненно,
Если будет надо,
и я умру за Африку мою !

Living in neighborly circumstances,
Of people's understanding and warmth,
I sensed with all my being,
That, since childhood,
Peoples of the world have found their voice.
She, Russia, had protected me.
I, existing on equal terms with the age
Didn't notice that the shoots
Of the coming Africa had sprouted in me.
And I will stand up for Russia's honor.
And this will be my highest reward.
But, beyond all doubt,
If it becomes necessary,
I too will die for my Africa!

Finally, James wrote poems about wartime, his father, childhood, and personal relationships—and because his gift is more lyric than epic, these are among his best.[89]

James's work is quintessentially Socialist Realist in one particular way. He traveled widely throughout the Soviet

Union and abroad to Africa, Europe, and the US, producing for each of his collections a substantial number of "location poems"; this travel occurred as a result of his membership in "writers' brigades," as they were still called in the late seventies, friendship societies with African countries, and groups of performing artists sent to enlighten and entertain workers in remote areas of the country. The visited places inspired a description of a historical event, a famous personage who lived or visited there, or workers in construction, mining, or fishing.[90] This rationalized input-output model of geographical creativity was not always successful. The James Patterson of the Soviet era was a man of his time who made compromises in navigating a repressive system while striving to attain his fullest potential.

Patterson's Pushkin

In the official nineteenth century cultural coding of the Russian empire, Aleksandr Pushkin served as a complex metaphor for imperial hybridity, the delicate process of assimilating diverse peoples into a coherent whole of "Russianness," and the same was later true of the Soviet Union with its own fraught nationalities policy.[91] Additionally, for the Soviets, from the 1920s onward, Pushkin's African heritage and his reputation as the poet of freedom in a repressive tsarist society was useful in establishing cultural-ideological ties to both African Americans and Africans. Both codings ("the other is who is one of us" and "our Russian-African brother") are relevant to James Patterson's official career, but for him, there was much more. His most multifaceted, satisfying, and genuine negotiation of identity came through a lifelong self-identification with Pushkin, whose maternal great-grandfather, Abram, or Ibragim Gannibal, was an African boy possibly from an area bordering Lake Chad, a gift to Peter the Great. Gannibal went on to have a distinguished but at times difficult public career under successive rulers. Pushkin is present in James's first poetry collection and in every collection through the last in 1993.

Occasionally, James uses Pushkin citations and epigraphs in his poetry, but more importantly, Pushkin's poetry is his life companion as it is to many other Russians. In "Pod sen'iu lipovykh allei …" ["Under the Canopy of Linden Avenues"], quoting from Pushkin's "K Iazykovu" ["To Iazykov"], James writes of Gannibal's (and Pushkin's) association of Africa with freedom during their difficult years and appears to apply the same to his own circumstances: "Россия, думаю о ней/ И снова повторяю это:/ … Он думал в охлажденны лета/ О дальней Африке своей …" ["Russia, I think of her/ And again repeat this:/ … In the cold years/ He thought about his distant Africa …"].[92]

For James, Pushkin is most importantly his brother-poet, always superior but also the bearer of potentiality. Thanks to Pushkin, black heritage models not victimization but the singularity that creates genius in "Razgovor s gipsovoi maskoi poeta" ["Conversation with the Plaster Death Mask of the Poet"]: "Вас не догнать, но понемногу/ Я, может, многих догоню" ["I can't catch up to you, but little by little,/ perhaps I can catch up to many others"]. This is, of course, the same as 1930s African-American and later African celebrations of Pushkin as potentiality.[93] True to form, James focuses on the geography and historical materiality of Pushkin's life, which he has made his own to the smallest detail in location poems. The apprehension of Pushkin is concrete, almost conversational, like that of a close acquaintance.[94]

Pushkin had a very serious interest in his family history, especially the Gannibal side, as in "Moia rodoslovnaia" ["My Genealogy,"1830] or the unfinished *Arap Petra Velikogo* [*The Blackamoor of Peter the Great*]. He saw his ancestors, Abram Gannibal, who was a military engineer and, under Elizabeth, became the head of the engineering section for the entire country, and Abram's son, Ivan, a famous military leader, as men of stature who served their country with honor. In his writing, James Patterson has a similar interest in both sides of his family but especially his father's. In 1964, he published *Khronika levoi ruki* [*Chronicle of the Left Hand*], an edited version of his grandmother Margaret Glascoe's family history and autobiography, translated and published in Russia in 1937 with Gorky's approval and now supplemented by a few pages of James's comments. (The original English-language manuscript has never been found.) The book was republished under James's name alone, not his grandmother's, both a clever career move prior to admission to the Writers' Union and reintroduction of a worthy text to Russian readers. James later searched for other family materials in the US, and his 1985 memoir, *Dykhanie listvennitsy*, included additional fragments of family history.

Like Pushkin and his two prominent ancestors, James saw his father as one of the generation of giants, such as Langston Hughes and Paul Robeson, those who had the courage to break with their accustomed worlds and set off into the unknown toward a new life. In "Poliu Robsonu" ["To Paul Robeson"], Robeson's voice reminds James of his father's: "Ваш звучный голос […] / То он суровый, то такой нежный,/ Каким был голос моего отца." ["Your rich-sounding voice … sometimes stern, sometimes so tender, as was my father's."]

James was separated from his father at the age of eight. In a poem about WWII soldiers, of himself he adds, *"Ia ranen smert'iu ottsa"* ["I'm wounded by my father's death"]. He mentions his father in almost every collection and praises his strength of character (*"nepreklonnyi moi otets"* ["my indomitable father"]) and will to action, and therefore wants to see *himself* both as an Abram Gannibal wandering near the place where Peter founded the Russian navy ("Брожу я по местам Залесским,/ как новоявленный арап Петра,"["I wander around Pereslavl'-Zalesskii,/ Like a latter-day blackamoor of Peter"]) and as a similarly strong personality:

"обжигался ... об известье о гибели ранней отцовской./ Зато в себе вырабатывал характер бойцовский./ Не избегал лишений,/ от трудностей не укрывался./ Пускай обжигался, зато никогда не сдавался."["I was burned ... by the news of Father's early death/ but developed a fighting character, didn't avoid privations, didn't hide from difficulties./ I may have been burned, but never gave up."] The self-heroicizing posture in these poems refers to the trauma of his father's early death, the privations of his WWII childhood, and various personal and probable career difficulties; but it is also the wishful thinking of a lesser second generation living in the relative comfort and stability of the Stagnation Era.

Through Pushkin, James united his two ancestries in productive fashion: "Сливались воедино два дыханья,/ природы русской и саванны дальней" ["Two breaths flowed together,/ Russian nature and the distant savannah"]. The identification with Pushkin gave James a spiritual home, uniquely his own, that allowed him space in the definition of "Russianness" that stood apart from little Jimmy, the face of racial tolerance in Russian society, and James Patterson, the cultural face of foreign policy toward Africa, but was rather James Patterson, the face of the poet. In a recent interview, he exclaimed, "I wouldn't be who I am without him," and on the door handle of his room he keeps a small flag stenciled with Pushkin's image.[95]

James and Lloyd Patterson's life experiences present the story of two generations of a black family that undertook the construction of a new identity in Soviet Russia. Transgressive vis-à-vis the land of his birth, Lloyd Patterson found authenticity as an icon of the policy of racial tolerance in his adopted country. As a native-born black Russian, his son James faced a more complex negotiation of identity in the vexed figuration of the brotherly other as authentically Russian, a cultural ambivalence illustrated in this article by cinematic representations of black Russians in Soviet and post-Soviet Russia. In his life journey, James shifted from political conformity to sincere, albeit ideologically convenient, identification with African peoples, finally locating his own Russianness in artistic identification with Aleksandr Pushkin.

Rimgaila Salys
Professor Emerita of Russian Studies
University of Colorado Boulder

James Lloydovich Patterson:
A Life in Pictures

138

Figure 1. The home of Patrick Hager, his wife, Sarah, and their children stood in the rolling hills of Nelson County, Virginia. *"I would go to the [Young] Pioneer camp and tell the kids about Snake Hill in Virginia. There was a log cabin where my grandmother Margaret's family lived."*

Figure 2. Margaret and her son Lloyd's house at 157 Liberty Avenue, Westfield, New Jersey. The house and others in the area were torn down for the construction of Brightwood Park in Westfield.

Figure 3. *"My father grew up in New York City and lived in New Jersey until he was twenty-one. He went through all sorts of hardships, like his parents before him."*

Figure 4. Langston Hughes and twenty-one colleagues head to Moscow to participate in the film project *Black and White*. Front row from left: Mildred Jones, Louise Thompson, Constance Wright, Katherine Jenkins, Sylvia Garner, Dorothy West, Margaret Lewis. Second row: Wayland Rudd, Frank Montero, Matt Crawford, George Sample, Lawrence Alberga, Langston Hughes, Juanita Lewis, Alan McKenzie. Third row: Ted Poston, Henry Lee Moon, Thurston Lewis, Lloyd Patterson, Loren Miller. Not pictured: John Hammond and Homer Smith. SS *Europa*, June 14, 1932. "My dear Mr. Patterson ... we have a fine group assembled to go, including Langston Hughes, and I shall also be in the party. I hope that you too will join us." Letter to Lloyd W. Patterson from Louise Thompson, Corresponding Secretary, Cooperating Committee for Production of a Soviet Film on Negro Life, March 24, 1932.

Figure 5. *"My father had a careful and sensitive attitude to his own children and friends. He rendered help at any minute. I rested on Daddy's knees with great delight, listening to his Russian speech mixed up with English words. He was implacable. He played piano superbly and was an unrivaled dancer. Daddy never missed an opportunity to play basketball. It was his favorite game. I watched with pride as he played. It seemed to me that he could be the best professional sportsman. He was a remarkable American, a man of great soul, extraordinary honesty; a man of duty and great responsibility."*

Figure 6. "On June 10, 1934 I arrived in Moscow. By force of habit I expected that the white people there, as everywhere else, would treat me with hostility. But to my joy, I found just the opposite. In my eighteen months' stay in Russia I have accomplished more than I ever dreamed I could do." Margaret Glascoe, "Negro Mother, Now a Shock-Worker" in *Sixty Letters About the Soviet Union,* collected by N.S. Rosenblit and R. Schuller (Moscow: Cooperative Publishing Society of Foreign Workers in the USSR, 1936), 10-14.

144

Figures 7 and 7a. At age three, James is cast in Grigori Aleksandrov's classic Soviet film *Tsirk* [*Circus*]. Aleksandrov's wife, Lyubov Orlova, plays James's mother. James and his "movie mother" remained close until Orlova's death in 1975. *"I was three years old, and I wasn't speaking. I remember Solomon Mikhoels took me for a walk in the garden so I would know him and behave for him in the film. After the war, he was killed by Stalin in Minsk. It was terrible."*

Figure 8. *"I am in the gymnastics display with my father on parade in Red Square. I only made one movie, and I became a movie star! I was an ordinary boy in an extraordinary movie."* Moscow, 1936.

Figure 9. *"I saw my grandmother Margaret as a child and heard the echo of her old sewing machine. She sang American spirituals beautifully in her low, deep voice. Grigori Vasilyevich [Aleksandrov], when he saw her, even forgot about his wife, Lyubov Petrovna [Orlova], for a while. He wanted her to play my grandmother in the movie. My grandmother held an important post in the NAACP. 'What will they think when they see me on the screen? No!' she exclaimed. 'I am already a grandmother!'"*

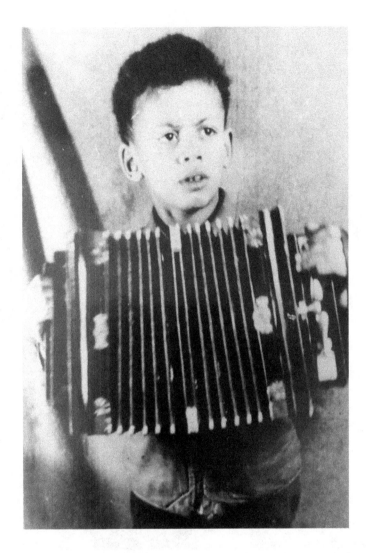

Figure 10. *"I went to the Gnessin Academy of Music. I don't remember why I am playing this instrument! My father was a great musician and played the piano. He knew Duke Ellington in New York and loved music. I learned the cello. A little! Later, when my mentor Mikhail Svetlov was sick in the hospital, I wrote a poem about the cello for him. The cello stayed with me, and my poetry was like the cello."*

Figure 11. *"When I was a little boy, we spent our summers in a rented house in Bakovka near Moscow. The elderly owner of the place, a naval veteran, had fought in the Tsushima battle and won the St. George's Cross. He used to hold me in his lap and tell me breathtaking episodes from his life. He never thought I would catch his passion for the sea and someday would be standing on the upper bridge, wrapping my sou'wester around me against the weather."*
Left to right: Lloyd Jr., the veteran, and James, 1938.

Figure 12. *"My father wanted us to have American names. He was afraid he couldn't pronounce Russian names. Everyone called me Jimmy. I was the oldest and an example to my brothers. We were different. Tom's mind was technical, I was serious, and Junior, more artistic. We loved each other."*
Left to right: Lloyd Jr., Tom, and James in Bakovka, 1938.

Figure 13. Vera Aralova Patterson with her sons James and Tom in Bakov-ka, 1938. *"Childhood scenes come to mind—all mischief done at an age when the unknown has a haunting power. You do what you like, and come what may."*

Figure 14. The family at a census taker's office in Moscow. A poster of Stalin appears on the wall. Left to right: unknown woman, Lloyd Jr., James, Lloyd, unknown woman, Vera, and Tom.

Figure 15. *"This painting has great significance for me. Mother succeeded in depicting our family at the moment of the great grief that had befallen us. Sorrow is perceived in our faces and poses. My grandmother was the embodiment of affection. I had never been cold during the most severe frosts. I am pictured without mittens, which I seldom put on. This is the last thing I keep in my memory about the war, about Sverdlovsk [Ekaterinburg] and my father."*

Figure 16. Nakhimov Naval School, Riga. *"I wished the girls I knew could see me in this outfit. I often went out to the courtyard of our school to play football. I decided to make my own leg guards. I tied books to my legs and went into the yard. A large wooden bat flew into my legs. If there were no book guards, my legs would have been broken."*

Figure 17. Lyubov Orlova pays twelve-year old James and the Nakhimov cadets a surprise visit. *"She was extraordinary."*

Figure 18. James studies at the Naval Academy in Leningrad and serves as a three-star lieutenant on a Soviet submarine. *"The commander of our submarine at first openly expressed indignation that one of his officers was writing poetry. He even wanted to throw me overboard. I don't know how it would have ended if I hadn't saved the ship. I was the officer of the watch, and I was scanning the horizon with a periscope. I remember that something was bothering me. I saw the outline of a deadly danger looming in the misty haze. Because I saw this, we averted our submarine."*

Figure 19. The brothers Lloyd Jr., James, and Tom. *"We were just guys!"* In 1960, Lloyd Jr. died in a car crash. *"Junior asked me to go with him and a friend in a car. I said no, that I had to work. It was horrible when Junior died in the crash. I think about it all the time. Mother was in Leningrad, and I had to tell her."*

Figure 20. *"The famous singer Paul Robeson and my father were close friends. On the several occasions when Mr. Robeson appeared in Moscow, he always came to our place. He and my father talked well into the small hours, recollecting the old days. Later, I didn't miss a single concert, and at some, the singer pointed at me in the audience, saying, 'This boy's father and I come from the same township in New Jersey.'"*

Figure 21. Leningrad Stadium, 30th Anniversary of *Circus*, 1966. *"Whenever Orlova addressed the public, she always found unique, heartfelt words. She referred to me as her 'movie son.' Many more concerts came later, in which we appeared. She was ageless. You never could tell her age, but I could by her hands."*

Figure 22. During James's writing career, he traveled to cities, towns, and villages throughout Russia to read his poems and meet fans. *"A lot of women came to hear my poems. I wondered if they really were interested in my poems, or me!"*

Figure 23. On August 17, 1988, James and Tom visit Komsomolsk-on-Amur for the dedication of a plaque to honor their father, Lloyd. *"In this city, my father died after a severe concussion received during an air raid on Moscow. The Nazis jammed our radio broadcasts, and to avoid this, my father and other commentators were sent to the Far East. My grandmother in America could hear her son's voice. Unfortunately, this didn't last long. She listened to all his transmissions. They suddenly stopped. I'm absolutely sure she was a suicide. How could she live after that?"*

Figure 24. The plaque for Lloyd Patterson is on the exterior of the Komsomolsk TV Center, the former broadcasting home to the All-Union Radio Committee.

Figure 25. *"I was married to Irina Tolokonnikova, a teacher and poet. In the mid-1990s, Mother decided that she and I should live in America. Irina did not want to go. I said to Irina, 'If you want your freedom, I will give it to you.' We were divorced."* Moscow, c. late 1980s.

Figure 26. *"Tom came to visit Mother and me in Washington. We went to Los Angeles to see our friend Frances Williams. We had not seen her since we were little and she stayed with us in Moscow. She passed away shortly after our visit."*

Figure 27. Vera and James sit in front of a painting by Vera, Washington, DC, 2000. *Self-Portrait with Sons* shows Lloyd Jr., Vera, and James in costumes of the commedia dell'arte *Pierrot and Harlequin*.

"To My Mother-Artist"

Perhaps you'll listen to what I say.
My irreplaceable,
You're in heaven.
As it turned out,
You passed away
A couple of days before
September eleven.

Figures 28 and 29: The grandmothers: Vera Grigorievna Aralova, photograph, 1915. Margaret Glascoe, portrait by Vera Ippolitovna Aralova Patterson.

Russia and Africa

Of myself I have no recall,
No memory of any details.
A famous child actor?
There too memory fails.
But I do recall
The tender songs they were singing,
Those two grannies over a cradle gently swinging.
And the way they bent over me, different of skin,
So much akin and yet not akin.
The swing of their arms was the same,
Their simple warmth was the same.
One sang songs from the land of my birth,
The other a lullaby of the American earth.
And there I lay,
Blessed with their sound.
Their grandson, their only one.
Of myself I have no recall,
No memories of any details,
But I do remember the tender songs they were singing.
Russia and Africa, over a cradle gently swinging.

Figure 30. *"I celebrated my eighty-eighth birthday with my friends. It was a wonderful time for me."* Left to right: *Chronicle of the Left Hand* publishing-team members Anna Lawton, Amy Ballard, Allison Blakely, and Cheryl Ross. James Lloydovich Patterson sits in front, holding a birthday gift of *Robinson Crusoe,* his favorite book.

"I was close to dying. My friends brought me back to life. I have all I need."

Acknowledgments

I am grateful to my friends Allison Blakely, Rimgaila Salys, and Amy Ballard for their contributions to my book. I also thank Jennifer Sunseri for her translation of *Chronicle of the Left Hand*, Andryusha Kuznetsov for his translation of my poem at the beginning, and Tatiana "Tanya" Boian, who provided her notes from oral histories. Although my granny's exact birth year remains a mystery, Romy Taylor's messages to Amy about the year and other important information were received with gratitude.

I thank Cheryl Ross for taking on the painstaking editing of my book. Her talent is an art, and I am appreciative of her work.

To Sasha Razor, I am indebted. She wrote an article about *Circus* and me. Because of that, people have come back into my life and I have made many new friends.

I felt like a movie star when Katya Chilingiri Balaban photographed me for the project. I thank her. It had been a long time since I wore a suit. I wore it with pleasure.

I am grateful to Anna Lawton of New Academia Publishing. She is responsible for putting my book in print. I have long dreamed of having a book published in the United States and in English. I hope that, full of feeling, the reader will take in this work, filled with the story of my granny Margaret and the nearest and dearest to me remembered.

Today, I have wonderful friends who help me and visit me, especially now that I am in the twilight of my life. It is a miracle. Thank you.

James Lloydovich Patterson
Washington, DC
February 2022

Notes

1. African-American writer Lorraine Hansberry (1930-1965) is best known for her play *A Raisin in the Sun*.
2. Legal documents use the spelling Hager or Hagar.
3. Patrick Hager's family lived near Massies Mill, Nelson County, Virginia.
4. Based upon death certificates, marriage licenses, and census documents, Margaret could have been about two years old.
5. It is possible that descendants of Daniel Higginbotham lived at Soldier's Joy Plantation, Wingina, Virginia.
6. "This all happened before Grandma Margaret was born" was added to provide clarity.
7. "Back before my family members moved to the cabin atop the mountain, before I was even a seed in my mother's belly" was added to provide clarity.
8. This is Margaret's quote.
9. "Though our family had Mr. Boyd to thank for employment" and "the man who bailed Pa out of jail" were added to provide clarity.
10. Likely, this is Margaret's quote.
11. Although legal documents show different birthdates for Margaret, an examination of the records shows that 1882 is most likely her birth year.
12. This is Margaret's quote.
13. While the text states that Margaret's father decided to send her to Washington to live with Signora Hunter, it later states that Margaret moved into Hunter's house in a "small place" that was "not far from" DC. We speculate that she may have meant not far from downtown Washington.
14. Likely, this a reference to Alma, Virginia.
15. Benning is a neighborhood in northeast Washington, DC.
16. "In Washington" was added to provide clarity.
17. This quote was attributed to "Cornelius Troup" in the Russian version of the book.
18. "One night, an episode would prompt me to no longer keep quiet about what had happened" was added to provide clarity.
19. "I told her what the son had attempted to do to me" was added to provide clarity.

20 It is very possible that this sentiment is an embellishment as it is in-consistent with other things Margaret says (and shows) she feels else-where in the text. It may have been added by others involved in the editorial process long ago.

21 Patrick Hager is buried in Oak Hill Memorial Gardens in Massies Mill, Virginia. His headstone shows a birthdate of November 5, 1817, and a date of death of April 5, 1899.

22 Born in Sweden, Joel Emmanuel Hägglund (1879-1915) moved to the US and took the name Joe Hill. He was a member of Industrial Workers of the World and wrote poetry and songs about the labor movement. In 1914, he was found guilty of murder in Utah. Although there were many protests about what many thought was a trumped-up charge, Hill was executed in 1915.

23 The marriage certificate shows that Margaret and Archie married on July 27, 1905, in New York City.

24 Based on research, Archie Patterson was likely doing contract work for a construction company.

25 "His death devastated me, but I had to keep going" was added to pro-vide context. The reported sentiment comes from conversations with Margaret's grandson James Lloydovich Patterson.

26 Records show that she was likely in her thirties by this point.

27 Lloyd would have been eight years old at this point.

28 While the text infers that Lloyd was fifteen not long after his fami-ly's move to Westfield, the original story text reads as if he was much younger than that at that time. This does raise questions about when exactly the Glascoe family moved to New Jersey.

29 Hampton Institute was added to provide context.

30 The "Great Depression" was added to provide context.

31 In 1931, nine black youths were falsely accused of raping two white women in Alabama.

32 Italian-born Salvatore Tonci (1756-1844) spent most of his life in Rus-sia as an artist.

33 Though the text states "More than three years had passed," in fact only two years had passed.

34 "I then took a train to Moscow" and "at the station" were added for clarity. Letters show that Margaret disembarked in Leningrad and took the train to Moscow, where Lloyd met her.

35 Based on records, Margaret may have been in her early fifties.

36 After this Moscow bombing, Lloyd visited his family in Sverdlovsk (Ekaterinburg) for three days. He was on his way to a new job with Radiocomitet in Komsomolsk-on-Amur in the Russian Far East. Af-ter several months, he died from the injuries he received in Moscow.

Margaret listened to his English-language broadcasts, and when she no longer heard his voice, she knew something was wrong. Her son's death destroyed her, and she died a few years later. Her grandson James suspects that she took her own life.

37 Prospect Mir is a main thoroughfare in the suburbs of Moscow. The famous Exhibition of Achievements of National Economy (VDNKh) is located there. The 1937 sculpture *Worker and Kolkhoz Woman*, perhaps better known as the logo of Mosfilm, is nearby.

38 The main campus of the University of Mississippi is located in Oxford, Mississippi.

39 The 1958 Battle of Maxton Field, North Carolina, between the Ku Klux Klan and the Lumbee Indians, inspired Malvina Reynolds to compose "The Battle of Maxton Field." Shortly after that, Pete Seeger sang it at Hootenanny concerts at Carnegie Hall.

40 Resistance hero Manolis Glezos participated in the Greek resistance movement against the Nazis during World War II.

41 In 1932, one black visitor to the Soviet Union estimated that "several hundred Americans of Negro race have been in Russia since the revolution." Dillingworth Dilling, "What Are the Opportunities of the Soviet Union?," *Abbott's Monthly* (June 1932): 6.

42 I am indebted to Allison Blakely, Julia Mickenberg, Romy Taylor, and the two readers for their thoughtful comments. I also owe thanks to Edith Clowes, Tim Riggs, Christian Douglass, and Kurt Schulz.

43 Margarita Glesko, *Dvoinoe iarmo* (Moscow: Profizdat, 1937), 127; Chatwood Hall (Homer Smith), "Soviet Hotel Decorated by Hampton Grad," *The Chicago Defender* (11 May 1940): 4. In this article, Hall writes, "Mr. Patterson was once expelled from Hampton for participation in a mass student strike, but was later reinstated after the resignation of Dr. Gregg as president." The student strike at Hampton Institute occurred October 8-18, 1927, and was motivated by various grievances, including the administration's harsh treatment of students and the college's lack of black teachers. Louise Thompson, a new member of the faculty who sided with the students, wrote a letter about the strike to W.E.B. Du Bois, resigned from Hampton the following year, and subsequently embarked upon an activist career. (See anonymous letter to Du Bois 10 Oct. 1927 and Louise Thompson 17 Oct. 1927 letter to Du Bois, in *The Correspondence of W.E.B. Du Bois*, Vol. 1, ed. Herbert Aptheker [Amherst: University of Massachusetts Press, 1973], 360-63). The magazine *Crisis* covered the strike and published part of Thompson's letter in December 1927. Lloyd Patterson participated in the strike with other students but was not one of its leaders. His school records show that he was continuously enrolled, except for

a brief period of seven to ten days during the strike. (School records information provided by Romy Taylor.)

44 Chatwood Hall, 4.

45 7 Apr. 1932 Louise Thompson letter to Lloyd Patterson, in Dzhems Patterson, *Dykhanie listvennitsy* (Leningrad: Lenizdat, 1985), 66.

46 For details of the film project, as well as the circumstances surrounding its cancellation, see Langston Hughes, *I Wonder as I Wander: An Autobiographical Journey*, introduction Arnold Rampersad (NY: Hill and Wang, 1993), 69-99; Faith Berry, *Langston Hughes: Before and Beyond Harlem* (Westport, Conn., 1983), 154-71; Allison Blakely, *Russia and the Negro* (Washington, DC, 1986), 93-6; Woodford McClellan, "Africans and black Americans in the Comintern Schools, 1925-1934," *The International Journal of African Historical Studies*, Vol. 26, No. 2 (1993): 382-84; Arnold Rampersad, *The Life of Langston Hughes*, 2nd ed., Vol. 1 (NY: Oxford University Press, 2002), 242-54; Kate A. Baldwin, *Beyond the Color Line and the Iron Curtain* (Durham and London: Duke University Press, 2002), 96-98; Glenda Elizabeth Gilmore, *Defying Dixie: The Radical Roots of Civil Rights, 1919-1950* (NY and London: W.W. Norton & Company, 2008), 144-46.

47 Louise Thompson Patterson, "Louise Thompson Patterson Memoirs: Trip to Russia—1932," draft 2, October-November, 1994, 7, qtd. in Baldwin, 266.

48 Lloyd Patterson letter to Margaret Glascoe, c. 1933, qtd. in Margaret Glascow, "I Am Among My Own People in My Own Country," *The Negro Worker*, Vol. 5, Nos. 7-8 (July-Aug. 1935): 33.

49 Glascow, 34. In the poem "Podsolnukhi Komsomol'ska," James Patterson describes gray-haired Margaret listening intently to her son's radio broadcasts to the US during the war. Margaret did not enroll in a university and returned to the US permanently c. 1937.

50 The circumstances of the meeting, as well as those of Lloyd's death, exist in several versions. On the couple's first meeting, see Al'bert Plaks, "Vechnyi mal'chik i vechnaia mama (Mal'chik iz 'Tsirka')," http://kackad.com/kackad/?p=2783&print=1 (accessed 25 Aug. 2013). The same version is in Leonid O., "Po prozvishchu 'Afrika'," http://www.persons56.ru/article/63 (accessed 12 Aug. 2013); see also Sergei Babaev, "Otets i syn," http://artek-kms.ru/otets-i-syn (accessed 11 Jan. 2014).

51 Thyra J. Edwards, "Hampton Graduate Holds Unique Post in Russia," *The Chicago Defender* (National edition) (1 Dec. 1934): 1; Chatwood Hall, "Hampton Grad Stands Out as 'Red' Painter," *The Chicago Defender* (National edition) (23 May 1936): 12. Langston Hughes wrote: "Long, tall Patterson who paints houses had married a girl who paints

pictures, and together they have executed some of the finest decorations for the May Day celebration." Langston Hughes, "Moscow and Me," *International Literature* no. 3 (July 1933): 63.

52 According to one source, James was born in Zagorsk, where the family lived before moving to Moscow, http://www.kopeika.org/articles/view/4562 (accessed 17 Feb. 2014).

53 "Podvodnik poet," *Sovetskii flot* (9 June 1957), qtd. in "Nash Dzheims Patterson." James later used some of this material, initially submitting an essay on Harriet Tubman as part of his application to the Gorky Literature Institute. (I am indebted to Romy Taylor for this information.) On Fort-Whiteman's final years, see Gilmore, 150-54; Joy Gleason Carew, *Blacks, Reds, and Russians* (New Brunswick, NJ, and London: Rutgers University Press, 2010), 179-83; and Harvey Klehr, John Earl Haynes, and Kyrill M. Anderson, eds., *The Soviet World of American Communism* (New Haven, Conn.: Yale University Press, 1998), 220-26.

54 P.A. Butov, "Mologvardeiskaia ulitsa. Molodogvardeiskaia, 6," http://e-butov.ru/content/page.php?id=77 (accessed 29 Dec. 2013).

55 Irving R. Levine was born in 1922 and began reporting from Russia only in 1955. Williams has apparently confused him with some other reporter living in Moscow at the time.

56 Frances Williams, "Slow Boat to Moscow," 4 Sept. 1986 interview, John Oliver Killens papers, box 50, folder 7: 1-5, Manuscript, Archives, and Rare Book Library, Emory University. In a later interview, Williams confuses Eisenstein with Grigorii Aleksandrov but mentions being on the set of *Circus* with Jimmy and teaching Orlova English. She also gives a more genteel version of Lloyd Patterson being tossed by the Soviet crowd, saying that his pants split during the toss (Frances Williams, "To Hell with Bandanas," oral history transcript, 1992-93: 131-32, 124, Bancroft Library, University of California, Berkeley, https://archive.org/details/tohellwithbandan00will (accessed 3 Jan. 2014).

57 Richard Alibegov, "Nash Dzheims Patterson. Nakhimovets, shturman PL, kinoakter, poet …," http://flot.com/blog/historyofNVMU/352.php?print=Y (accessed 11 Oct. 2013).

58 Butov. The other English-language announcer was American communist Ann Stanley. Various accounts of Lloyd Patterson's death circulated for some time: The *Chicago Defender* reported that he died of spinal meningitis in Moscow in 1942 (Anonymous, "Hamptonite is Dead in Russ Capital" (28 Mar. 1942): 2; According to Frances Williams, during a 1970s visit to Moscow, Vera Aralova told her that she had just come out of their building when it was bombed during the war and her husband did not survive the German bombing raid (Frances Williams, "Slow Boat to Moscow," 10).

59 Marina Kuz'mina, "Mesta zatoptannykh mogil," 2007 pdf, p. 20, at marinakuzmina.ru (accessed 5 Dec. 2013).

60 See "Zdanie, gde v filiale mezhdunarodnoi redaktsii rabotal Lloid Patterson, diktor, internationalist," http://wikilovesmonuments.ru/monument/9415/ (accessed 27 Nov. 2013).

61 Kesha Fikes and Alaina Lemon, "African Presence in Former Soviet Spheres," *Annual Review of Anthropology*, Vol. 31 (2002): 517.

62 Alibegov.

63 Elena Varshavchik, "Vypusk 'Modnye istorii' rassylki 'Moda i my' ot 03 oktiabria 2009 goda," http://content.mail.ru/arch/80927/3533004.html (accessed 12 Nov. 2013); also Iren Andreeva, "Odezhda na luchshee," http://www.confection-expert.ru/frearticles/?artid=23 (accessed 11 Jan. 2014).
    A short biography and four Vera Aralova works are available at www.artpoisk.info (accessed 11 Jan. 2014); one additional portrait (*Tat'iana Metaksa*) is on ArtLib.ru.

64 Vil'iam Savel'zon, "Rossiia i Afrika peli," 21 May 2013, http://орск56.рф/index.php?option=com_content&view=article&id=3237 (accessed 4 Aug. 2013).

65 Vladimir Konstantinovich Grabar', "Nash Dzheims Patterson. Nakhimovets, shturman PL, kinoakter, poet …"

66 The collection is named after one of the bays of the Kuril Islands.

67 Nikolai Aleksandrovich Veriuzhskii, "Nash Dzheims Patterson. Nakhimovets, shturman PL, kinoakter, poet …"; Seva Novgorodtsev, "Ostorozhno, liudi!," 16 March 2010, http://www.seva.ru/bb-seva/?id=1423 (accessed 12 Aug. 2013).

68 Karen Kossie-Chernyshev, "Reclaiming 'D. Patterson' (J. Patterson), Child Star in Grigori Alexandrov's *Circus*: A Reconstructive History," *Sound Historian*, Vol. 8, 2002: 68-9. According to Al'bert Plaks, Orlova studied Lloyd Patterson's heavily accented Russian for the Marion Dixon role and he would supply her with necessary English words during filming. James wrote about the filming of *Circus* in the poem "Posviashchenie aktrise."

69 James Patterson's change of profession was fortuitous: he was retired in 1958 as part of a reduction in naval forces (Vladimir Konstantinovich Grabar', in "Nash Dzheims Patterson").

70 1963 *Rossiia-Afrika* [*Russia-Africa*]; 1964 *Khronika levoi ruki* [*Chronicle of the Left Hand*]; 1973 *Rozhdenie livnia* [*Birth of the Downpour*]; 1978 *Vzaimodeistvie* [*Interaction*]; 1980 *Zimnie lastochki* [*Winter Swallows*]; 1984 *Zaliv dobrogo nachala* [*Bay of Good Beginning*]; 1984 *Krasnaia liliia* [*The Red Lily*]; 1985 *Dykhanie listvennitsy* [*Breath of Larch*]; 1989 Gulistan Mat'iakubova, *Prekrasnoe chuvstvo* [*Wonderful Feeling*]—Patterson's translation of Uzbek poetry; 1993 *Nochnye strekozy* [*Night Dragonflies*].

71 The composition of the painting is based on Kandinsky's "Lady in Moscow" (1912) but omits its esoteric elements.

72 Both the Plaks and Anatolii Filatov accounts remark on Vera Aralova's infantilization of James in the absence of a father. See Plaks and Anatolii Filatov, "Negritenok iz kinofil'ma Tsirk," http://www.proza.ru/2008/05/24/66 (accessed 28 Dec. 2011).

73 James Patterson is one of the subjects of Yelena Demikovsky's forthcoming documentary *Black Russians: The Red Experience.* Red Palette Pictures.

74 As a corollary of attention to children's welfare, as expressed in *Circus*, there later appeared the continuing filmic motif of the adoption of the victimized black child into the Soviet family. Older Russians remember fondly *Maksimka* (dir. Vladimir Braun, 1952), a popular film from their childhood, in which an abused African boy is rescued from an American slave ship and, after various peripeties, is adopted as an *iunga*, or ship's boy of the fleet, by Russian sailors. Maksimka's adoptive father, the sailor Luchkin, is played by Boris Andreev, an actor who since the 1930s had been typecast as the brawny, sometimes flawed, but ultimately all-Russian good guy, thereby enhancing the motif's mythic charge.

75 For more on the film, see Rimgaila Salys, "*Stiliagi* or Wear Those Green Socks," *KinoKultura* 50 (October 2015).

76 Aleksandrov preserved the conventional Soviet image of American blacks by insisting that Jimmy be dressed in thick black tights (clearly visible in the iconic photo from *Circus* of Dixon and Martynov holding Jimmy) so that he would appear more black.

77 On *Circus* see Rimgaila Salys, *The Musical Comedy Films of Grigorii Aleksandrov: Laughing Matters* (Bristol, UK, and Chicago: Intellect Press, 2009), 121-200.

78 Dzhems Patterson, *Dykhanie listvennitsy*, ill. between pp. 64-5.

79 Vladimir Grabar', "Nash Dzheims Patterson."

80 Carl Shreck, "Jim Patterson: Black Soviet Icon's Lonely American Sojourn," *The Moscow News* (24 June 2013), reprinted http://02varvara.wordpress.com/tag/african-american/ (accessed 13 Feb. 2014).

81 Shreck.

82 Shreck.

83 *Volshebnyi krug* was the first of a popular two-part series. Ideological principles were typically conveyed more directly and overtly in Soviet children's films.

84 A. Mitta, "Kogda ozhivaiut graviury," *Iskusstvo kino*, 11 (1976): 102, 104-05.

85 On racism in Russia during these years see Charles Quist-Adade,

"The African-Russians: Children of the Cold War," in Maxim Matusevich, *Africa in Russia, Russia in Africa: Three Centuries of Encounters* (Trenton, NJ: Africa World Press, 2007), 154-73.

86 Maxim Matusevich, "Africans in Russia," http://www.encyclopediaofafroeuropeanstudies.eu/encyclopedia/africans-in-russia/ (accessed 1 Dec. 2013); Sergey Mazov, "Soviet Policy in West Africa: An Episode of the Cold War, 1956-1964"), in Matusevich, *Africa in Russia*, 295.

87 Karen Kossie-Chernyshev, "Reclaiming 'D. Patterson' (J. Patterson), Child Star in Grigori Alexandrov's *Circus*: A Reconstructive History," *Texas Oral History Association*, Vol. 8 (2002), 69; Ivan Poltavskii, "Zanimatel'nye istorii. Iz materialov zhurnala NVO "FARVATER Submariners" 1 (17) 2011, http://www.farvater-submariners.com.ua/patterson.html (accessed 4 Aug. 2013).

88 The phrase is a borrowing from Pushkin's "Chaadaevu." Versions of the "lesenka" line, a borrowing from Mayakovsky, were common in 1970s verse.

89 See for example: "Rossiia i Afrika" and "Podsolnukhi Komsomol'ska."

90 For example: "Borovsk" (visiting the village where Tsiolkovskii worked as a schoolteacher), "Sekvoia" (Lincoln visited the forest of giant trees), "Serengetti" (visiting where Hemingway once reread *The Sevastopol Tales*).

91 Catherine Theimer Nepomnyashchy and Ludmilla A. Trigos, "Introduction: Was Pushkin Black and Does It Matter?" in *Under the Sky of My Africa. Alexander Pushkin and Blackness.* Ed. Catherine Theimer Nepomnyashchy et al. (Evanston, IL: Northwestern University Press, 2006), 33.

92 See also: "Bernovskii omut," "Ne znaete vy," and "Boldinskaia osen'."

93 See Olga P. Hasty, "The Pushkin of *Opportunity* in the Harlem Renaissance," in *Under the Sky of My Africa*, 226-47. James Patterson is pictured with Pushkin's death mask in Mike Edwards, "Pushkin," *National Geographic* magazine, Vol. 182, No. 3 (September 1992): 61.

94 See "V Krivokolennom pereulke," "Poplyvu ia iz Opochki," "Kol'tsa," "Domik niani," "Malen'kii Pushkin gostit v podmoskovnom imenii u svoei babushka Mar'i Alekseevny Gannibal," "Samovar Oleninykh."

95 Shreck.